THE LIFE OF TILKEPNAYE: A 12 MONTH STUDY OF NATIVE CHALDEAN CATHOLICS IN THEIR HOMETOWN OF TILKEPE

By Fr. Michael J. Bazzi

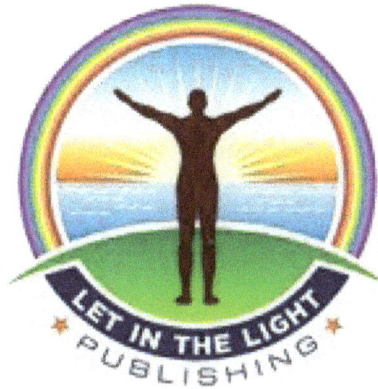

San Diego, California

2021

www.letinthelightpublishing.com

Edited by Sally Ades

Cover by Amy Grigoriou

© 2021, Let in the Light Publishing, in collaboration with Bazzi Publishing

Library of Congress Control Number: 2020920501

ISBN# 978-1-941464-42-7

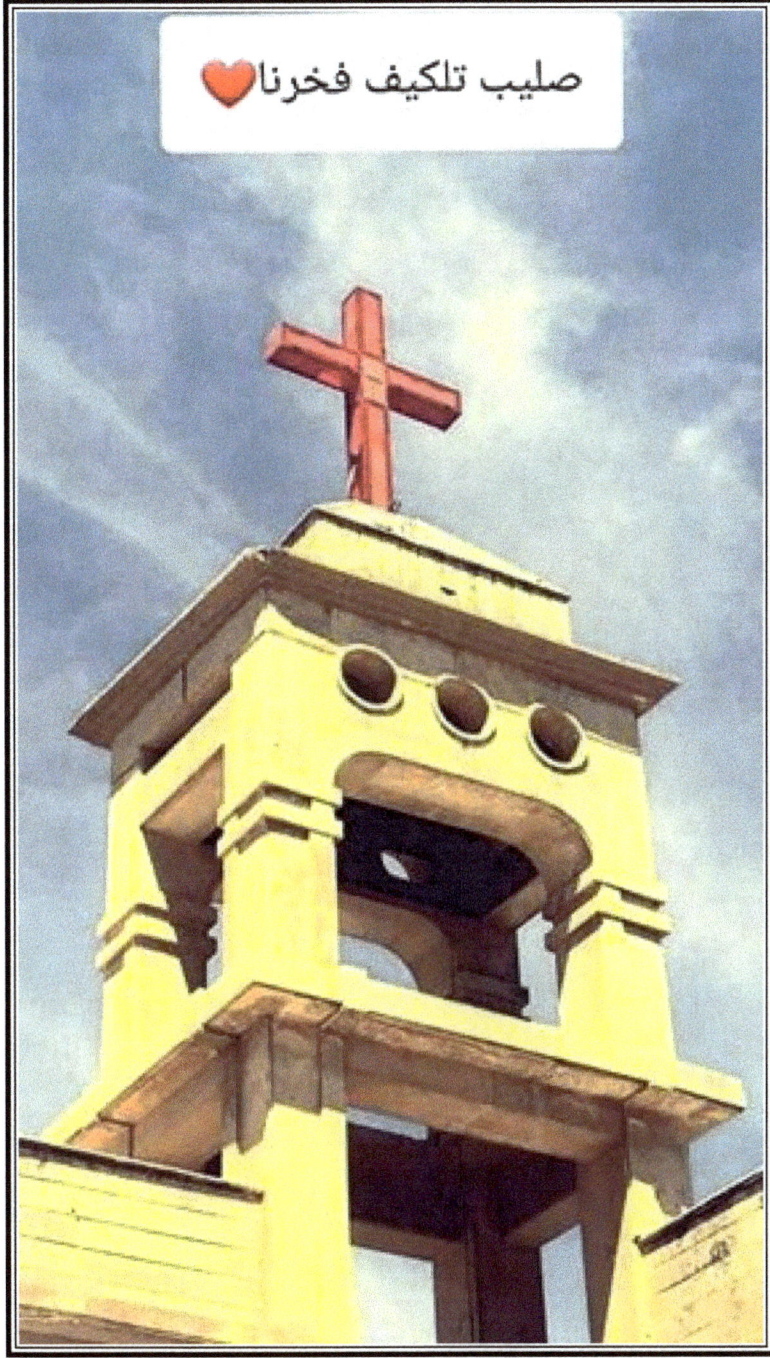

صليب تلكيف فخرنا ❤️

ܨܠܝܒܐ ܕܝܠܟ ܦܪܩܠܢ ܨܠܝܒܐ ܕܝܠܟ ܦܪܩ ܠܢ ܨܠܝܒܐ ܕܝܠܟ ܒܬܪ ܗܫܐ ܦܪܩ ܠܢ

صليبُك خلَّصَنا، صليبُك يُخلّصُنا، صليبُك سـيُخلّصُنا

YOUR CROSS SAVED US, YOUR CROSS IS SAVING US,
YOUR CROSS WILL SAVE US

Table of Contents

Oh Tilkepe, you are honey in my mouth	Oh land of my father and mother
Your name I bear within me	your soil I mix with my blood
Tilkepe doosha b-kimmee	Ya athra d-babi w-yimmee
Shimmakh bta-ninne immee	Uprakh bgolinne b-dimmee

PREFACE

I invite you, dear reader, to come with me to my beloved city of Tilkepe to get to know the daily way of life of its indigenous Chaldean Catholics, who lived in it. We will take a close look at how they celebrate holidays, seasons, weddings, and religious, social and economic customs and practices on a monthly basis throughout the year. I have divided the book into twelve chapters. Each chapter examines one month. I explore some of the things that were happening at Tilkepe, and I bring back the unforgettable memories of everyone who lived in it. I hope that others will join me in writing and expanding the limited literature available today, so that all these memories remain a treasure in the heart of all the faithful Tilkepnaye, keeping them connected to their beloved city.

For your information, because the letter P پ does not exists in the Arabic language, the Arabs called our city Tilkaif, rather than Tilkepe. Tilkaif means the city of pleasure, so Tilkepe's true meaning was misunderstood and lost. The correct translation of Tilkepe is "Hill of Stones." In the Aramaic language, it is made of two syllables, Til (Tilla), which means hill, and kepe, which means the stone. Thus, Tilkepe means the hill of stones. With the intention of keeping the original meaning of the city's name alive, I will use the original Aramaic name of Tilkepe, and I will refer to its native people as Tilkepnaye in my Aramaic language—in the Chaldean dialect (Swadaya-vernacular). I regret not using the name Tilkepe in the 1969 Arabic version of my previous book, which in Arabic was called "Tilkaif, تلكيف it's Past and Present." It is important that the correct Aramaic name and meaning is known and never forgotten.

During our visit, we will follow the lives of the Tilkepnaye, who lived in the last half of the twentieth century. We will follow their roles and discover in each season and month the practices of their daily lives, how they were led by their Christian Catholic faith, and the crystallization of all aspects of their behavior. We will look at how Tilkepnaye raised their children and how they conducted their relationships with each other and with non-Tilkepnaye.

I published this book in three languages for the benefit of the old and the young. This book is especially for those who cherish the fact that they are Tilkepnaye, but were not fortunate enough to be able to visit or reside in Tilkepe. The words "native Chaldean Catholic" has a different life and meaning to those who have lived in it for generations. I have found that this deep connection to the city is unique to the native Chaldean Catholic and is difficult to detect in those who immigrated to the city in recent years. In the past thirty years, people of different religions and nationalities have immigrated to Tilkepe.

Since 1989, I have been offering Aramaic Chaldean language classes at Cuyamaca College in El Cajon, California. In one lesson, I asked students about their city before they came to America. I was glad to be in a class with students from all over northern Iraq. However, one of them mentioned that she was born in Tilkepe, but she refused to be called Tilkepnaitha! (meaning feminine, singular, native from Tilkepe). I was moved by the answer, and this prompted me to call the natives Tilkepnaye (plural form), a distinction from modern immigrants.

At Cuyamaca College, classes are taught for three semesters, and each semester has its own textbook. The textbooks are written in Chaldean and English. The second book, along with grammar, includes 20 recitations. It tells about the customs practiced by the Tilkepnaye and the people of the villages of the Nineveh Plain. It was from this that I drew the information in this book. Who would have predicted fifty years ago that Tilkepe would be completely emptied of its families, and its people would be scattered northward?

The Islamic State of Iraq and Syria (ISIS) expelled the Tilkepnaye from their city, but neither these terrorists nor those following their example can remove the name Tilkepe from their hearts. Let everyone know that in 1972, I left Tilkepe for Rome to study and I took its soil with me wherever I traveled, whether in Italy or in America. It is still with me and will remain under my pillow as long as I am alive.

On the day that ISIS invaded Tilkepe, I entered the church and prayed for my loved ones and other persecuted people. Immediately, I remembered the Lamentations of Jeremiah the Prophet, when Jerusalem was destroyed in the Babylonian Exile in 587 BC. His words apply to Tilkepe: "How alone sat the city. Crying at night, crying and tears on her cheeks. She has no lover from all her lovers. Remember, O LORD, what has become of us, has become our inheritance to strangers. Our homes for foreigners. We became orphans without a father. Our mothers are widows. O Lord, send us back to thee, and we will rejoice. Renew our days as old times" (Lamentations 5:1-3, Peshitta).

The terrorist organization Islamic State (ISIS) invaded Tilkepe for three days beginning on Wednesday August 6th, 2014, the same day as the Feast of the Transfiguration. Once conquered, ISIS presented three options to Tilkepe Christians: either convert to Islam, death by beheading, or pay tribute. In addition, ISIS confiscated all the Chrsitians money and property. In stark contrast to the treatment of Christians, the mosques of Tilkepe welcomed the Muslim invaders over the loudspeaker with, "Allahu Akbar (God is most great)." Christians were forced to leave and flee to the north. Meanwhile, the evil ISIS wrote above the doors of the Christian homes the Arabic letter N, ن indicating that the residents of this house are the followers of Jesus of Nazareth.

The Islamic State did not have mercy on the young or old, women or men, or pregnant women. They spread terror, injustice, displacement and enslavement in every place that they seized. When the wicked ISIS invaded Tilkepe, they propagandized from the Qur'an with the following slogans. Surah al-Tawbah 9:29: "Fight those who believe not in Allah nor the Last Day, nor hold that forbidden which hath been forbidden by Allah and His Messenger, nor acknowledge the religion of Truth, (even if they are) of the People of the Book, until they pay the jizya with willing submission, and feel themselves subdued." Also, Surah al-Tawbah 9:14 was quoted: "People of the Book (Christians and Jews) who do not accept the religion of the truth (Islam), until they have paid tribute (penalty taxes) by hand, being inferior."

In addition, the following quote from Surah al-Ahzab 33:26 was used to justify the actions of ISIS, "And those of the People of the Book who aided them - Allah did take them down from their strongholds and cast terror into their hearts. (So that) some ye slew, and some ye made prisoners." Further, Surah al-Ma'idah 5:33 reads, "The punishment of those who wage war against Allah and His Messenger, and do mischief in the land is: execution, or crucifixion, or the cutting off of hands and feet from opposite sides, or exile from the land."

Chilean poet Pablo Neruda (1904-1973) paraphrased the early Chaldean Church leaders when he wrote: "You may cut the flowers but you cannot stop the spring." An archaeologist who visited Tilkepe in 1840 AD conducted excavations on the hill. As the whole hill was a cemetery, the archaeologist only managed to collect a number of pottery fragments. Tilkepnaye had started burying their dead on the historic hill in the beginning of the ninth century AD. On March 2, 2015, ISIS destroyed the cemetery of Tilkepe. They burned homes, used churches as archery fields, and used Mart Shmuni's Shrine, outside the city, as a mortar launcher.

The Iraqi army on November 22, 2016, liberated the city from the hands of ISIS. On January 19, 2017, Tilkepe was completely liberated. On September 18, 2017, the Iraqi army forces moved approximately 3,000 women and children to Tilkepe (1,573 Iraqi women and 1,324 foreign women).

On Thursday, January 26, 2017, leading the people of Tilkepe, Mar Louis Saco, the Chaldean Patriarch, celebrated the historic moments of the raising of the Holy Cross on the dome of the Sacred Heart Church. On January 20, 2018, Mar Louis Saco, the Chaldean Patriarch, held the first Mass in the Church of The Sacred Heart in Tilkepe after its liberation.

For four years, Tilkepnaye could not visit nor bury their dead in the cemetery. On March 1, 2019, in the midst of a destroyed cemetery, Friday prayers for the dead were recited under the leadership of Father

Shaher Nuri Shadhaya, the pastor of the Church of Tilkepe.

Sacred Heart Church in Tilkepe numbered 7,100 people in 1968. The native Chaldean Catholics had 5000. The old Eastern Church had 500. The Assyrian Church had 1,200 people and regional Christian transplants accounted for the remaining 400.

The following information was sent to me on February 14, 2020 by Mr. Sefian Jerboa: Currently in Tilkepe there are 28 native Chaldean Catholic families with 82 persons. These families are from the following tribes: 1- Hakim 2- Zora 3- Zinglo 4- Puta 5- Shathaya 6- Rafooly 7- Shamoo 8- Kurico Bazzi 9- Bawa 10- Jadaan 11- Rabban 12- Arabo 13- Mikha 14- Salmu 15- Aggos 16- Sitto 17- Geezy 18- Jarboa 19- Goro. (These 19 tribes have other branches. That is why there are 28 families) Besides the Native Chaldean Catholics, there are 30 families of Christian brothers with 60 persons, who immigrated to Tilkepe recently.

The number of Christians has decreased significantly in Tilkepe for political, security, economic reasons and because of the deportation, intimidation, and displacement practiced by ISIS and their associates. There is lack of basic services in the restored areas, despite the presence of security. Homes, churches, and places of worship still have not yet been rebuilt. The need for removing the remnants of destruction, such as mines, and for fixing badly needed electrical repairs are still being ignored. That is why most of them do not want to return to their dear and beloved town.

Evening Prayer (Ramsha – Vespers)

Tilkepe, the beautiful city	Loved by all of us
As it is filled with relatives and friends,	it fills our hearts
Tilkepe matha khleetha	Min kullan eelah b-eetha
Mnashawatha w-khooreh mleetha	W-bgo libban eela dreetha

FOREWORD

The native Tilkepnaye, the Chaldean Catholics mixed a life of faith with everyday life. They had annual and monthly customs of feasts and festivals, which made life so beautiful and a joy to be in this world. This went right along with their faith in Christ, the Son of God - who is the Way, the Truth, and the Life - and their honor to his mother the Virgin Mary and the martyrs and saints. They kept the teaching of the Chaldean fathers and teachers of the Catholic Church. All these made them enjoy this world while they were awaiting the joy, which never ends in the world to come, in the heavenly kingdom. Liturgical seasons and prayers were at the heart of life of each Tilkepnaya.

THE CHALDEAN LITURGY

The prayers of the liturgy of the Chaldean Church are collected from the writings of the apostles and the disciples of Our Lord, and from the Old Testament and the New Testament in the Holy Bible and from the writings of the holy Chaldean Fathers, especially in the year of Our Lord four hundred and ten. At the synod (council) of St. Isaac and St. Marotha, they collected the prayers of St. Addai and St. Mari, and St. Simon the son of dyers and St. Jacob of Nisibin and St. Ephram the harp of the Spirit and other Chaldean teachers of the first four centuries of Christ. In the seventh century A.D., the Chaldean Fathers arranged the Chaldean liturgy in the monastery of Daira Alaya in Mosul in the time of the patriarch Eashuayab Hthayyawaya, A.D. 658 .

All Chaldean Christians start the beginning of the New Year on the Feast of the Circumcision of Our Lord, on the first day of January. The churches of the East, and among them the Chaldean Church, start the liturgical year at the beginning of the month of December.

THE LITURGICAL YEAR OF THE CHALDEAN CHURCH

The liturgical year of Chaldeans summarizes the plan of God in the history of Salvation in one year and fills twelve months, and has these seasons: (a) Annunciation (Advent), four Sundays; (b) Birth (Christmas), two Sundays; (c) Epiphany, eight Sundays; (d) Fast (Lent), seven Sundays; (e) Resurrection (Easter), seven Sundays; (f) Apostles (Pentecost), seven Sundays; (f) Summer, seven Sundays; (h) Elijah: seven Sundays, but the season of the Cross starts from the fourth Sunday of Elijah (four Sundays parallel with the last four Sundays of Elijah); (i) Moses, four Sundays; (j) the Consecration of the Church (the final season), four Sundays. At the end of the last week of this season, the liturgical year ends.

THE LITURGICAL PRAYERS

Chaldean Christians pray every day just as Our Lord commanded: prayers of evening, and of night, and morning. Jesus said in the Gospel of Mark 13:35, "Watch, because you do not know at what time your Lord will come. Perhaps at evening or at the middle of the night or toward dawn." In the evening prayer service, believers thank God for his blessings to them on that day. At night prayer, they follow the words that Psalm 119:62 said: "In the middle of the night I arose to give you thanks because of your ordinances, O Just One." At Morning Prayer, believers thank God who raised them from the sleep of night, which is a symbol of death, to the light of day.

All prayers including Sunday prayers, feast days, and Memorial Day prayers (remembrances of the death of saints or the killing of martyrs) are placed in three books called prayer books. The first prayer book has the prayers from the day of the Annunciation until the Great Fast (Lent). In the second prayer book are the prayers from the Great Fast until the end of the season of the Resurrection (Easter). The third and final prayer book contains the prayers from the feast of Pentecost (the descent of the Holy Spirit) until the final Sunday of the season of the Consecration of the Church.

Every twelve months, Chaldean believers meditate on the holy mysteries of the Christian religion - from the time that God sent his Son, Our Lord Jesus Christ, to the world. He was born and baptized. He preached the truth of our Lord and for this, he suffered. He was crucified on the cross. He died and then he arose. He sent the Holy Spirit upon the apostles. They, with the disciples and the early Christians, spread the Catholic Christian religion through all creation. Many people and nations repented and were baptized.

In the last seasons, the prayers show us how at the end of the world the holy cross will appear. Elijah the prophet representing all the prophets, and Moses, the symbol of the Law and the commandments, will appear. The two of them confess that Jesus is the Messiah who came for the salvation of the world. Through him are fulfilled all the prophecies of the prophets of the Old Testament. After him, there is no prophet to come. On the Last Day, at the end of the world, Christ will come the second time to judge the living and the dead. When he comes, the holy Church will welcome him. She will be dressed in the clothes of a bride. She will greet him, with her children, with psalms and hymns. They all will live with him in the kingdom of heaven forever.

The language used by the Chaldeans is scholastic Aramaic. The Aramaic language appeared in Mesopotamia and east Syria, North of the Euphrates River, around the fifteenth century B.C. And during the rule of the Chaldean Emperor Nebuchadnezzar in the sixth century B.C., Chaldeans began to speak, to write and to pray in Aramaic with a Chaldean Dialect.

We know with certainty that Chaldeans inherited the Babylonian and Akkadian languages. Most of the vocabularies of those languages mixed with the Aramaic. Over time, through the mingling of the people of our nation with other people, foreign words entered into our Chaldean language. Chaldean Christians of Mesopotamia who live in the mountains (north) mixed with their language words of the language of the Kurds. For those who lived in the plains (south), the language of Arabs mixed into theirs.

For those who lived in Turkey, the Turkish language mixed with their language. Those who resided in Iran, Persian words mixed in with their speech. Therefore, the modern Chaldean Aramaic language is not pure Aramaic, like the classical language. It is not always easy for Chaldeans from the mountain to understand Chaldeans of the plain.

We encourage every Chaldean faithful to honor his heritage and to learn and to teach Chaldean Aramaic. Aramaic was the language, which was spoken by our Lord Jesus Christ and His mother, the Lady Mary, and the holy apostles.

THE 22 LETTERS (CONSONANTS) OF THE ARAMAIC – CHALDEAN ALPHABET

ܝܼܗܒܝ ܘܥܘܕܝܡ ܒܘܬܘܬܐ ܕܠܝܫܢܐ ܐܪܡܝܐ – ܟܠܕܝܐ

١	ܐ	ܐܵܠܲܦ	A		١٢	ܠ	ܠܵܡܲܕ	L
٢	ܒ	ܒܝܬ	B		١٣	ܡ ـܡ	ܡܝܡ ܘܡܝܡ (ܡ)	M
٣	ܓ	ܓܵܡܲܠ	G		١٤	ـܢ	ܢܘܢ ܘܢܘܢ (ܢ) (ـܢ)	N
٤	ܕ	ܕܵܠܲܕ	D		١٥	ܣ	ܣܸܡܟܲܬ	S
٥	ܗ	ܗܹܐ	H		١٦	ܥ	ܥܹܐ	AH
٦	ܘ	ܘܵܘ	O		١٧	ܦ	ܦܹܐ	P
٧	ܙ	ܙܝܢ	Z		١٨	ܨ	ܨܵܕܹܐ	SS
٨	ܚ	ܚܝܬ	HH		١٩	ܩ	ܩܘܦ	Q
٩	ܛ	ܛܝܬ	TT		٢٠	ܪ	ܪܝܫ	R
١٠	ܟ	ܟܵܦ	E		٢١	ܫ	ܫܝܢ	SH
١١	ـܟ	ܟܵܦ ܘܟܵܦ (ܟ) (ـܟ)	K		٢٢	ܬ	ܬܵܘ ܘܬ ܘܬ	T

Chapter 1
THE EVENTS OF DECEMBER
THE MONTH OF GOOD NEWS

This month in the liturgy of the church is a month of joyful annunciations.

Tilkepe, the beautiful city	Loved by all of us
As it is filled with relatives and friends,	it fills our hearts
Tilkepe matha khleetha	Min kullan eelah b-eetha
Mnashawatha w-khooreh mleetha	W-bgo libban eela dreetha

All the Catholic Chaldeans pray the Tabrikat in honor of the Lady Mary. Some who are able to go to church after vespers pray the Tabrikat together. Those who are not able to come to church gather at night after supper at the house of one of the relatives. Little ones and adults gather around the large manqal (mud made container) filled with wood or charcoal, brought by the charcoal trader from the mountain. After the Tabrikat prayer, they tell stories, fables, and parables. They grill oak nuts, and they drink tea with cardamom or with cinnamon, which exudes a distinct aroma through the entire house.

Each Sunday of the month of December, Catholic Chaldeans remember one of the four announcements of the gospel, the ones that were announced by the Angel Gabriel. On the first Sunday, the Chaldean liturgical rite reminds us of the announcement of the joy which the angel gave to Zechariah and his wife, Elizabeth. He announced to Zechariah that they would have a son in their old age. On the eighth day of this month occurs the feast of the Lady Mary, conceived immaculate ("of unstained nature"). On the second Sunday, the Church remembers the announcement of Our Lady, the Virgin Mary, when the angel said to her, "You will be with child and will give birth to a Son and you will call him Jesus." On the third Sunday, the Church remembers the joy of Zechariah and Elizabeth at the birth of John the Baptist. Lastly, on the fourth Sunday the liturgy speaks to us about St. Joseph the Righteous, about when the angel announced and said to him that the Lady Mary is a Virgin, and she conceived by the power of the Holy Spirit. When the angel left Joseph, he took her to his house. He allowed her to guard her virginity until his death. In addition, she kept her virginity, and she knew no man until her Assumption from this earth to heaven in soul and body.

CHRISTMAS

In this month, some Tilkepnaye fast from dairy products and meat for twenty-four days. There are some who fast seven days, some who fast three days, and some who fast on the day before the feast of Christmas. During the week before the feast of Christmas, Chaldeans make flatbread and kuleche (bread filled with rice and raisins), and they sew or they buy new clothes and they prepare charazeh (roast mixed nuts), oranges, and sweet lemons.

In the evening of the small feast (i.e., Christmas, as opposed to the great feast of Easter) people, hear (attend) the great vespers. They wait until midnight Mass. The alleys of the town shake from the voice of the well-wishers who cry out in joy, "The Lord is born," and the respondents say "Glory to his name." Before the beginning of the Mass, they burn torches in the yard of the church before the manger of the Baby Jesus.

After Mass, they return in a hurry to the house and the mother takes out from the tanureh (the stewing jar) of kraeh (i.e., beef tripe, barley, and sheep intestines filled with rice and ground beef). They sit down and eat happily after midnight, and in the morning they distribute charazeh, oranges, and money for small children. On the day after Christmas, all the alleys of the town are filled with brides who slept during the feast day in their "fathers'" (parents) homes. The brides would return to their husbands, carrying their clothes in bundles, singing, "The feast is over and there is no more mindaneh (another word for charazeh). We are going to be stuck with the in-laws." (Zelle aidha wmidaneh, Zeelukh balukh b-bi khimyane).

From the early times until the beginning of the twentieth century, Tilkepnaye lit their houses with the light of a lamp of linseed oil or olive oil. However, after the first quarter of the twentieth century, they began using oil lamps, lanterns they filled with fuel and lit them. In the beginning, for cooking in paya (small mud oven), they used to burn dry cow dung and dry sheep dung. For the baking of bread in the tanureh (large oven for baking bread), they burned hay and straw. However, from the second half of the twentieth century, electricity emerged into all homes and gave light, fire (heat) for cooking and heating cold water, and radio, telephone and the computer.

THE FARMERS OF TILKEPE

In the month of December, rain, lightning, and thunder are heard everywhere. The cold air and long, dark nights make people go inside and keep themselves safe in their houses. Many of the farmers and sowers were not able to sow in the summer, and waited until the moisture moistened the ground enough. When the moisture from the surface of the ground reached the moisture of the soil of the bottom of the ground (i.e., the water table). The sower was obliged to sow before the winter reached him.

The farmer in Tilkepe wakes up before dawn. The woman of the house prepares hot food for him: rishta and (fried) rishta (spaghetti), lentils and shopateh (lentils with meat and garbanzo beans). She would then put in his bag provisions for his entire day: bread and cheese and onions or jagig (blue cheese) and date syrup or grape syrup and dates or raisins. Before he starts eating, the farmer, or sower, puts out toona (hay) and barley for his beasts of burden, and he takes his equipment into the yard. He looks to the sky and he remembers the proverb of the fathers, "The red clouds in the evening twilight call the farmer to come and eat dinner. But the red clouds of the dawn send away the farmer from the yard." If from the early morning the clouds are not red, the sky will be serene and there is no danger of rain.

After one heavy meal in the morning, the farmer puts charokheh (leather shoes) on his feet and he puts a thick khameyseye (wool jacket) on his shoulders. He ties his trousers and wraps sosekyatha (piece of cloth) on his arms. He goes to the yard and he leads out his beasts of burden: donkeys and she-donkeys or mules and she-mules or workhorses and she-workhorses. He saddles his animals and he puts the plow, the plowshare, and the yoke onto one animal.

On another animal, he puts the rest of the farm equipment and the juharat (bag) filled with hay. On another animal, he puts the seeds. He takes with him a sower with his apron. The farmer, the sower, and the beasts of burden go together before the sky lights up. They turn their faces toward the field. They pray and put their day in the hand of the Lord God.

In the1950s, games popular among young people were the games of cuts, soccer, nets, weightlifting, heels and others. The game of cuts involved two teams. The goal was to "cut" behind the other team. When "cutting" was done successfully, players on the opposing team had to sit out. The game continued until all the players on one team were out.

In addition, among young women, game beads, jumping, and walking were popular. Game beads involved trading beads with the beads acting as currency. Jumping required one person to lean down as the other jumped over their backs. Walking often turned into a competition to see who could walk the fastest.

Members of the Legion of Mary (Circa 1965)

Chapter 2
THE EVENTS OF JANUARY
NEW YEAR AND EPIPHANY

The Christian New Year starts on the first day of the month of January. On this day Christian Chaldeans celebrate the feast of the Circumcision of Our Lord. Eight days after his birth, Our Lord named Jesus, whose translation means the Savior, was circumcised. Six days after the feast of the New Year, the feast of the Epiphany (i.e., the manifestation of Jesus to the world) occurs. When our Lord was age thirty, St. John the Baptist baptized him in the River Jordan. Most Tilkepnaye wait for this feast to baptize their children, and share with the joy of baptism of the Lord. After this day, Jesus started the three final years of his life, preaching and teaching until the crucifixion. He died, arose, and ascended into heaven.

MEMORIAL DAYS

After the feast of Epiphany, memorials of one or more of the martyrs and saints occur every Friday through January and February. The first Friday is dedicated to the memorial of the killing of St. John the Baptist. On the second Friday occurs the memorial of the martyrdom of St. Peter and Paul. On the third Friday occurs the memorial of the four Evangelists: Matthew, Mark, Luke, and John. The memorial of the martyrdom of St. Stephen occurs on the fourth Friday. On the fifth Friday occurs the memorial of the Greek Teachers (Fathers): St. Basil. St. Gregory and St. John and their friends. On the sixth Friday, the Chaldean Church remembers the memorial of the Syrian Fathers: St. Ephraim and St. Jacob of Nisibis. Also, on this Friday the Chaldean Church remembers the Roman teachers: St. Ambrose and St. Augustine and St. Jerome. On the seventh Friday comes the memorial of the patron of all the Chaldean Church, which is the memorial of one individual person.

Thursday before the eighth Friday, Tilkepnaye used to celebrate the Thursday of boozers. Before 1930 the young boys used to meet in the afternoon. They planned to go to all the roads leading to Tilkepe. To stop farmers coming back, the young people traditionally were allowed to take the donkey of the farmer. When the farmers reached the town, they gifted either chickens or a bottle of Arak or wine. As for the rest of the people, they were trying to get rid of alcohol (except the addicts!), so they fasted with repentance and prayer.

On the last - the eighth Friday - the Chaldean Church remembers those who died. On this day Chaldeans eat turnovers filled with either rice or dates, and after Mass the faithful go to the cemetery (lit., "home of tombs") to visit the dead and pray memorial prayers for them.

The Visit of the Bishop to the Church (Circa 1970)

Chapter 3
THE EVENTS OF FEBRUARY

The Chaldean patriarchs of the early centuries took care of the problem of the times and seasons. They were the first to understand and establish the very beginnings of astronomy. They were the first to understand the movements of the stars and the changes of the weather. They gave knowledge to the east and the west and the mountain (north) and the plain (south), for farmers and all workers of the fields, those who wait all year to plant and to harvest their crops and to bring their produce into the house.

Winter in Tilkepe starts in the months of October and November. However, the beginning of winter really is on the twenty first day of December. From that time, hard rains descend and Chaldeans of these towns jump for joy. Their hearts fill with happiness as plants begin to sprout. Ditches, swamps, reservoirs and wells fill with water. Moreover, people drink from them and also make their animals drink from them. Young men learn how to swim in them.

However, in the second quarter of the twentieth century, clean water entered the towns. Pipes were installed in houses, and many of the wells were shut off. With running water in the houses, the swamps became filled with soil, and cleanliness replaced the dirt. Various sicknesses like glaucoma and pests like lice and fleas were eliminated.

THE FEAST OF PRESENTATION OF JESUS TO THE TEMPLE

On the second day of this month of February, the Chaldean Church celebrates the feast of Old Simeon. On this day, the Church remembers Our Lord when he was forty days of age. Mary and Joseph presented him in the Temple in Jerusalem and Old Simeon carried him in his arms and blessed the Lord. Believers lit candles in the church and took them to the home where they lit them during hardships. One elderly man of Tilkepe told me about the stamp of the cross that they put on the candles. He had brought it to the Church of Tilkepe, from the traces of a church in Khirbet Askar located in the lands of Tilkepe.

FEAST OF THE ATONEMENT-BAOUTHA

Twenty-one days before the Great Fast, on the Monday that occurs after the fifth Sunday of Epiphany, the Chaldean Church holds three days of fasting of atonement, a time of asking forgiveness from God in penance and prayer. All Catholic Chaldeans fast three days from meat and dairy products. Some do not eat anything at all those three days. On the Thursday after the Day of Atonement, Chaldeans eat the sweets of St. Elijah, and this day is called the Thursday of Thanksgiving, the day of thanking God.

THE SIX SOUNDS IN CLASSICAL ARAMAIC

Due to the influence of neighboring languages, six of the twenty two letters were modified in sound in classical Aramaic: (ܬ ܟ ܓ ܦ ܕ ܒ) and were added to the alphabet. However, only four of the six letters (ܒ ܓ ܟ ܬ) were given new sounds while two of them (ܦ ܕ) for some unknown reason were pronounced like the letter (ܘ) waw = w (ܕ ܦ). Of the six modified letters, five were modified simply by adding a dot underneath the letter, and one (ܦ) by merely adding a semi-circle attached below the letter (ܦ).

Letter		6 sounds & their Pronunciation			Examples	
ܒ	b	ܒ	wa	ܗܳ	ܟܰܒܪܐ	man
ܓ	g	ܓ	gh	ܓܳ	ܦܓܪܐ	body
ܕ	d	ܕ	dh	ܕܳ	ܗܠܡܝܕܐ	student
ܟ	k	ܟ	kh	ܟܳ	ܡܐܟܠܐ	food
ܦ	pw	ܦ	wa	ܗܳ	ܢܦܫܐ	soul
ܬ	t	ܬ	th	ܬܳ	ܒܬܘܠܬܐ	virgin

These six sounds are expressed in one word BGaDiKPaTh

(ܒ ܓ ܕ ܟ ܦ ܬ) ܒܓܕܟܦܬ

Chapter 4
THE EVENTS OF MARCH
THE GREAT FAST (LENT)

In the month of March, the countryside is clothed with a green suit; the plants sprout up and fields start blooming. All the parks and territory are filled with lilies and wild roses of every color: red, blue, yellow, brown, black and white. The smell of greenery opens one's heart, and all creation becomes one voice, cries out to God, and says, "How wonderful are the deeds of your hands, O Lord!" Families that have animals are grateful for the young ones, which are born. The cows, mares, she-donkeys and ewes (female sheep) give birth. The nesting hen hatches her chicks, and the baby birds hatch. All these add beauty and sweetness to creation.

Spring normally starts on the twenty first day of this month, but in Tilkepe spring starts at the end of February. At this time, the seven weeks of the Great Fast of fifty days begin. Many Chaldean Christians do not eat meat all seven weeks. Some fast the first week and the last week, and they do not eat breakfast until midday. The food for these days is tahini and halawah (dough with sesame and honey), bread and green onion, lentils and chickpeas and gurgur (similar to cous cous) or barley cooked with onion and widow's stew, which is crushed onion with sumac and wild herbs from the field including urtica, Aqla d-deeka, and malva.

THE SHRINES

From the first Sunday of Lent until Palm Sunday, Tilkepnaye go out to festivals during the day after Mass. On Sundays during Lent, they celebrate each Sunday, and they honor one saint who has a shrine inside or outside of Tilkepe. The first Sunday is feast-Shaira of Mar Daniel. The second is of Boukhtsaada. The third is of Saint Shmouni. The fourth Sunday is of Saint John the Apostle. The fifth is of St. Joseph. The sixth is of Arbeeni (the 40 Martyrs).

Priests, deacons, and people go out to the shrine to hear the teachings of Christ and the preaching of the priest. After this there is folk dancing. Sellers of nuts and charaze (mixed nuts) spread out. Many young men race on stallions or mules or donkeys. People walk from the village to the place of the shrine, dressed in colorful clothing. Just like the river, which runs, the people are also coming and going. Some go walking and some ride animals. All of them are happy; all of them laugh and joyfully converse. Small children play hide and seek amongst families and strangers. People spend all day outdoors. Mothers carry food with them, loaves of bread and tahini and kulaycheh.

In addition, the families' of the groom's-to-be carry sheelane (food for the son's fiancée, a pan of yellow barley, colored with saffron), so they can eat together in the large yard of the shrine. At sunset, everyone returns to his house; his heart is open and joyful, filled with love and faith from the air and the sweet aroma of spring.

The Estrangela Letters ܐܣܛܪܢܓܠܝܬܐ Out of the 22 alphabet letters, the following six letters have different shape when writing in Estrangela

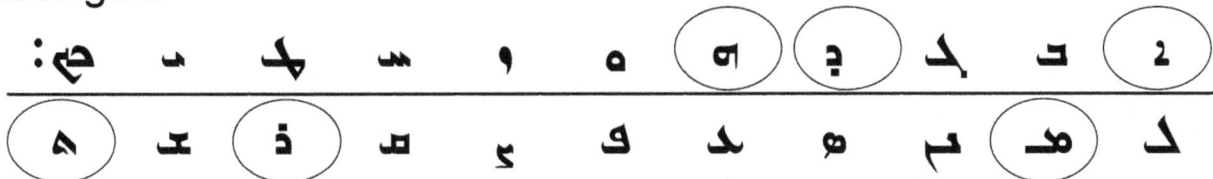

	Letter				Examples		
1-	a	ܐ	A	ܐ	ܐܒ		August
2-	d	ܕ	D	ܕ	ܕܪܐ		century
3-	h	ܗ	H	ܗ	ܐܠܗܐ		God
4-	m	ܡ	M	ܡ	ܡܪܝܡ		Mary
5-	r	ܪ	R	ܪ	ܪܒܐ		great
6-	t	ܬ	T	ܬ	ܟܠܬܐ		Jar

Chapter 5
THE EVENTS OF APRIL

Tilkepnaye wait for the air of spring and wild roses. The Great Fast passes in a flash, and people spend most of their days in the field. Some of them cut weeds like thorn bushes, pod trees and darnel. Others search for the holes of mice, and kill them with a pump (i.e., they smoke them out). Many small children go out and dig out truffles and lagneh (a wild, potato-like vegetable) and parsnip with a hoe. With their hands, they cut mushrooms and rooster claw and khnakhtasota (types of green leaves) and malva (bitter herds) and gurgaymeh (a wild berry).

EASTER

The feast of Easter occurs between the twenty-second day of March and the twenty-fifth day of April, as was ordered by the Fathers of the council of Nicaea in the year 325 of the Lord. On every Sunday of the Great Fast, Chaldeans celebrate the feast of one of the saints, but on the seventh Sunday comes the Feast of Hosanna (i.e., Palm Sunday). On the Saturday of Hosanna, they would prepare yellow loaves colored with saffron. All young children went to the church and there the priest divided them into groups. Some kids went with one of the priests or one of the deacons. Each group would take one alley of the village, and they would sing the songs of Hosanna. One of them carried the cross and another carried the banner. They took both the cross and the banner to every room in a house (i.e., to bless it). At the end of the blessing, people used to hand the priest, deacons and the little kids either money or nuts or eggs. On Hosanna (Palm) Sunday, the priest blessed the olive branches. Everyone carried the branches and took them to their fields. In every field, they put one of the blessed olive branches.

On Holy Thursday, all people went to confession and received Communion, and the priest washed the feet of the twelve disciples. During all Fridays of the Great Fast, people did The Way of the Cross after the prayer of vespers, but on the seventh Friday, the Passion Friday (i.e., Good Friday), Tilkepnaye fasted until midday and then ate bitter herbs, like rooster claw and khnakhtasota. In the evening, they attended the homily and then, they attended a procession with the cross and the tomb of Our Lord (i.e., a wooden box covered with black sheets, symbolizing the tomb of Christ). Many stayed awake all night in the Church. On the evening of the Saturday of Light (i.e., Holy Saturday) [so called because it was believed the Holy Spirit descended on the tomb while Christ was taking the dead to heaven], after the vespers prayer, they prepared for midnight Mass. At this time, the sacristan collects donation from those who want to share in the Virgin Mary passion.

Many who came to the church brought with them hardboiled colored eggs. After Mass, people broke the eggs and ate them. They returned to their houses, their hearts filled with joy, wishing each other blessings and saying, "The Lord is risen." The response is: "Blessed is his name."

On Easter day people play with boiled eggs. The head of the family lays out 10 or more eggs and asks each member of the family to pick up two eggs. They play by hitting their eggs against each other. The winner is the one whose egg does not break. The game continues until there is one person left with an unbroken egg.

First communion in Tilkepe 1964

THE FIRST COMMUNION

The nuns of St. Domenic along with the administration of the elementary school for girls in Tilkepe used to gather boys and girls in the building opposite the church (Qonagh) and teach them religious lessons and melodies. Tilkepnaye used to celebrate the first communion on the Friday ceremony of the Resurrection, the Friday of Confessors. However, later the church celebrated the first communion on the first Sunday after Easter in the presence of the Archdiocese Bishop. The beautiful scene of children wearing their angelic white suits is unforgettable. In addition, the children wait for gifts from family and relatives, and their hearts are filled with joy and happiness, a memorable day.

WEDDINGS

Tilkepnaye inherited the saying, "Prata traissar Gora yan qora," which is literally translated "When a girl reaches twelve years of age, either marry or be buried." In the first part of the nineteenth century, many marched according to this parable. Then things changed, as girls started to receive culture in primary, secondary, college and even university.

Engagement ceremonies started with personal contact by the young man's family and the young woman's family. Then there was the official announcement that the young man and his family visited the young woman. After agreeing on a dowry, the families officially announced the day of marriage which was usually in two or three weeks.

Until the 1940s, the matrimonial ceremony was performed at the home of the groom. Then it moved to the church. Most marriages were held on Sundays. Some married couples walked around with the family and relatives in the streets of Tilkepe and danced in the public squares. When the wedding party passed by near the house of some friends, they would offer Araq to those in the wedding. The wedding days for some were two or more days. The new Sunday (Khoshaba Khatha) was the first Sunday after Easter and was the day when the engaged, who were waiting for 50 days, had a period of great fasting. The courtyards of Tilkepe were filled with the wedding celebration.

Young Men Preparing to Plant Melon Seeds

Chapter 6
THE EVENTS OF MAY
HARVEST AND BUDRA

The Tilkepnaye who depend on the crops for their livelihood wait all year to harvest and bring their crops into their homes, to repay the debt that they incurred in the days of winter. The lending system in Tilkepe consisted not from borrowing from banks, but borrowing from wealthier villagers. In the month of May, when the sky gets warm, people take their bedding up to the roof. Little children run from roof to roof playing with each other. Relatives and older neighbors pass and cross over the barrier (between houses) to sit together and to drink and to tell stories and discuss the daily news. At night, supper is taken to the roof or balcony. The people of the house gather around the lagan or Sayniya and the Tabaq (large iron plates used to share meals) filled with bread, flatbread or loaves, with cheese or blue cheese, olives, tahini, or date syrup, if there is no cooked meal prepared. At 9 PM, the sacristan rings the bell so that all the people will pray the Angeles.

The joy of the relatives, the good outdoor air, sometimes the songs of drunk people, the drums or the horn of people who have an engagement or a wedding at home, marked the harvest season. Sometimes people use the bird ch-haly. Some youths hunt the bird this way: They would bring a large worm and pull a long, strong thread around it and put the worm on the ground near the garbage, waiting for the bird ch-haly to come down and pick up the worm. The thread would go around its leg and it would fall down, to be captured by the youth. At night, they make the bird fly. They tie a piece of cloth on his leg and they pour gas over it and tie it with wire, they burn the cloth and send the bird to fly. Moreover, all the children would cry out "That is, that is ch-ha-ly." All of these things made sleeping on the roofs a great and unforgettable time.

THE HARVEST SEASON

Many farmers harvest barley, lentils or fava beans and they collect cucumbers. The farmers and those who own fields hired workers who use to stand in the market waiting for work opportunities. They took them to work in their fields. All trails and roads and paths were filled during these days from those going and coming (lit., "goers and comers") to the work- especially, the sawaleh (the person who guided the donkey). They conducted their animals carrying shakhreh (which is two ladders with two humidors in the upper part, to form two sides of the equilateral triangle) filled with barley or lentils, and brought them to the threshing budratha (park on outskirts of the village). The Sawaleh returned time after time until the sunset. Sometimes, people were seen riding on a wagon pulled by a donkey or mule. They would be singing or praying. With them, the birds of the sky sang because some of the heads of the grain which fell from the shakhreh or from the ashafeh (wood for grain over the back of the animal) left much food for the birds.

The name of the Lord God and prayers were in the mouth of everybody because the farmers were bringing their crops, and workers were getting their wages. Many prayed the rosary while they walked, and they sang religious poems, stories, and ballads - especially the story of the Virgin Mary (called) "In the name of the Father and the Son." On the fifteenth day of this month, Chaldeans celebrate the feast of the Virgin Mary, the keeper of the fields. During these days, they request from the Mother of God, through her intercession toward Jesus her Son that all the melon patches and the fields will be safe from the qopta, the locust, grasshoppers, grain weevils, worms, scorching weather, and birds.

Secondary School Bible Study (1964-72)

College Student Bible Group Field Trip Near Tilkepe

Chapter 7
THE EVENTS OF JUNE
MELON PATCHES

Tilkepnaye who owned melon patches waited to pick cucumbers, melon, and squash. They took some of the harvest home and some was sold in the market and to neighboring villages and a portion was used for taking to the Gap (special location for selling of melons) in Mosul. They carried grain with the shakhreh, or in wagons or in flatbed trucks to budratha (park). They would start crushing garbanzo beans and they used the hay thresher for lentils, barley, and wheat. Every day in the evening, many prepared to go picking in the melon patch. They did this early in the morning. They rode their animals and they walked with the morning stars. Before sunrise is when they would reach the melon patch. In that place, there are already men sleeping at night on their hushatha (outdoor bed). In the evening, those men broke white marble and they made them into small pieces and put them by yellow melons and ripe melons. Before dawn, and with darkness still on the ground, those men and those who came from the house would start picking and cutting each melon, which had by its side a piece of white marble. They brought melons to the market in gunnysacks (guniyeh) or zabul, or they would leave them so that a large flatbed truck would come and carry them away. After that the youth were left to guard the garden. Anybody who tilled the land or built a booth (qupranaa) and guarded the melon patch or slept in the melon patch never forgot those beautiful days as long as he shall live. How beautiful it is when the owners of those patches gathered thistles, kessuk, and khata (both wild trees with thorns) and made a fire until they drifted to sleep, each one left to the hushe (bed of kesuk and khata) of his own melon patch.

In this month, the Chaldean church celebrates the month of the Sacred Heart of Jesus and the feast of Pentecost - the descent of the Holy Spirit on the apostles in the upper room in Jerusalem. In this month, schools close. Little children and young people help their families. Some gathered crops, some tilled the land and some harvested. Some guided the shakhreh. In addition, others watched the melon patches or picked the melons or cucumbers and carried them from the patch to the market or the house. On the other hand, they rode on the thresher. Work was available for boys, for girls, for men, and for women - even for those who are elderly. How beautiful it is, that the city became like an ant colony, with people going and coming (lit., "goers and comers") from everywhere. This month of blessings renews life in all the people. Those who waited all winter and spring now receive money in their money bags. They pay their debts, and they save for the weddings of their children, for building, for buying animals or lands, or for traveling to far lands.

Mill Stone for Grinding the Wheat

The Shrine of Mart Shmoony in Tilkepe

Chapter 8
THE EVENTS OF JULY
THE FEAST OF SAINT THOMAS

On the third day of this month, the Chaldean church celebrates the feast of St. Thomas the apostle, its patron, and the first who brought Christianity to Mesopotamia, then traveled to India, where he was martyred. Tilkepnaye on July 1st used to throw useless ceramic pots in the streets. This month, too, people used to rent and sell homes as the economic year began.

GARDENING AND HARVEST SEASON

In these days, vegetable patches gave all their blessings and slowly, but surely, the roots would start to dry out. There would be nothing left from the cucumber, except shlanka (the ripest cucumbers) for the seeds of next year. There were some people who gave their crops for the harvesters with the combine; they collected the crop with gunnysacks, and they carried it to the house or to the market for sale. There were others who gave their crops for harvesters, who used sickles and collected it with hooks, and then they brought it with shakreh to threshing floor. They crushed it with the garigra (a threshing instrument) and they winnowed it. They took the straw home in the khararat (black bag made from goat hair) for food, for the animals and for baking.

Each home had its own threshing floor. No one was able to carry his crops to his house until after the appraisal of the tax collector who gave him a bill, which obliged him to pay money to the government as soon as possible. With the appraiser and the tax collector came hundreds of poor people, whether from the village itself or from outside of it and each one of them carried sacks, and each owner of a threshing floor gave one or two handfuls of wheat, barley or lentils for the needy. In those days, people would bring fruit from the mountain region, such as grapes or figs, and trade them for wheat or barley.

In this month, carobs would dry out, and they became bajinjeh. Moreover, many small children would fill their bags with them. They took them to the street of the village and sold them by the bowl. Everybody worked and earned during this month. Life was so sweet. People forgot the heat and the hot wind of July.

Gas Vendor

Chapter 9
THE EVENTS OF AUGUST

THE FEAST OF TRANSFIGURATION AND THE ASSUMPTION

On the sixth of this month, the feast of the Transfiguration occurs. On it, people say the summer is going to end and the cool days are coming. On the fifteenth of this month, the Feast of the Assumption of the Lady Mary-soul and body to heaven-occurs. Some of the faithful fast nine days before the feast. They do not eat meat and dairy products. Nevertheless, they put suffra in their bread, which is made of roasted melon seeds and roasted garbanzo beans crushed together with sumac, mulberry, or sugar.

Tilkepnaye prepare for construction. Those who are stonecutters go out to work in their stone or marble quarries. From the stone quarry, they cut huge pieces of rock with the pickaxe. Then they put a piece of iron (i.e., an iron wedge) in a small opening in the middle of the rock, and they split it. When the rock resists, they blast (lit., "hit") with dynamite. They make a deep hole in the middle and they fill it with dynamite, and they place a fuse, and the dynamite shatters the rocks, and the stonecutters start to cut the rock into small pieces. They bring a donkey and they put a rock carrier on the donkey's back. They stack the broken rocks on the carrier. They carry them to the village for construction. From the limestone quarry, they would break fardata (limestone) into small pieces and take them to a furnace to bake them.

Plaster Coefficient Furnaces

There were clever people in Tilkepe, whose job was constructing furnaces. They would dig a wide ditch in the ground, build a small room on the ground out of bricks, and cover the furnace from the top. They would leave some holes so that the smoke would escape through them. They stacked the small pieces of limestone around and on the top of the furnace. They would light the furnace and start to feed (the fire), throwing the straw of the grain on it for a period of three days and three nights without stopping until all the limestone is baked. They waited two days until the furnace cooled and became cold. After that, they carried the baked pieces of limestone to the village. They put them into the stone mill, and then a mule went around, pulling behind him a stone wheel which was made of granite stone. After they crushed the limestone, they took it to one side, then sifted it, and took out the powder of the limestone for building and construction. They put it in a zabeera (basket made of branches) and carried it to a zabul (reed basket), and they brought it to the house that was to be built. The people of the house who have prepared to build would bring the mason, and with him the rock handler who gave him the rocks. With him also were mortar mixers. The house owners would invite neighbors and friends to eat barley soup with meat, and they would ask them to help them free of charge, especially those who lay the mortar.

People of villages would build rooms in the house, a living room and a porch. They would open windows and holes in the room. From inside they would build a loft, and in the back of the loft, they would build a closet or a storeroom. Underneath the loft, they would leave a basement for animals (bikare), and those who had money would put marble on the floor of the porch to make a court. Some rich people would have (separate) rooms for people, crops, and for animals. However, poor people had one loft, and the entire household would sleep upstairs, and from the same stairs that people use, animals would descend to the basement to their own manger or bikare. Between the door of the loft and the outer gate, and outer door, there was a courtyard with a tanureh (oven) for making bread and a paya (small oven) for baking.

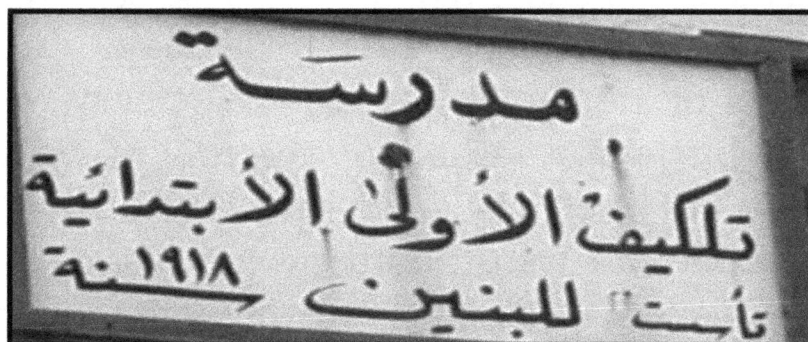

The elementary school for boys was established 1918

Chapter 10
THE EVENTS OF SEPTEMBER
THE FEAST OF THE CROSS

In the beginning of the month of September, the weather cools and people come down from the roof, fearful of the rain showers. In addition, the children prepared straw, candles, and muchekiatha (like a small charcoal container) and sticks for the campfire on the day of the Saturday of the Feast of the Cross. Every day, they carried ainabba (burning materials) through the streets. Each one of the young boys carried with him a taptapa (cow chips). They stacked cow chips over it, and they put straw or gas over that. All the little kids of the area gathered, and then they lit the cow chips of the ainabba.

The young man stood, and the people applauded, and they went around in the alleys until the fire of their taptapa extinguished. They will not be satisfied until they went to other kids who had an ainabba. When the Feast of the Cross approached, the roofs of the village were brightened with the fire of muchekiatha, the ones which were made of red mud, like small bowls filled with sheep droppings or burning wood.

All Catholic Chaldeans remember the Feast of the Cross, September 14, the day in which St. Helena, the mother of King Constantine, in the year of the Our Lord 321, gave money to the workers. While digging around the mountain of Calvary in Jerusalem, they discovered the living (true) Cross. On it, Our Lord was crucified. Because of the joy of Christians, they lit a fire at that time. The good news spread all over the eastern countries. This custom is followed in Christian countries (in the Middle East) until today.

On the night of the Cross Day, after electricity was introduced to Tilkepe, night prayers were held on the roof of the church, using loudspeakers, so the whole city could hear, and enjoy the melodious and fresh melodies that were heard by the priests' and deacons' voices. Also, on this day, Chaldeans remember the return of the wood of the cross 628 A.D. from the Persians, who on 610 A.D. invaded

Jerusalem and captured the Patriarch and with the wood of the cross, the Persians took the cross and the priests to Catesphone (Near Baghdad) in Mesopotamia.

PREPARATION OF FOOD

In the month of September, the Tilkepnaye prepare supplies for the entire year. Farmers had three seasons of planting. Some plant in summer, from the month of August until September. Others planted when the first rain came in the fall. Still others planted when the moisture flow flowed (para prayleh), from Christmas until the month of February.

In these times, people planted grain and barley. However, they planted lentils and fava beans at the time of the rain flow. In the month of April, garbanzo beans are grown. Melon and cucumbers in March. People planted two kinds of barley: the white kind and the other, black. The black they have nicknamed "local." The karoniya grain - they make out of them yellow gurgur (like cous cous). The khamrik kind of grain is used for white gurgur. Italian grain is used only for puqota (pearled barley). Almania grain and ketchla are used for bread and noodles.

Chaldeans of Tilkepe are very skilled in making gurgur. The people of the house bring home the grains, pick the small rocks out of them, boil them in a big pot, and dry them on the roof. Then after that, they take them to the stone mill to be hulled. After they finish hulling them, they carry them to the house. They put them in a hand mill or machine (i.e., to crack the grain), and then they sift them, and they make out of them the following: (a) gursa reshaya, (b) palgaya (medium), (c) qtaa wublaa("cut and swallow").

Concerning those who prepare puqota: The people of the house brought grain, and they picked the rocks from them again. They took them to the stone mill, removed the shell from them, and they put them in gunnysacks and brought them to the house. They took from them with a sifter: (a) puqota, (b) mbarghal, (c) gursa (the grade) below puqota, for kubaibeh.

On these days, all the members of the family worked. Women picked out the rocks and boiled the grain, and with them were all the girls and small children. The men carried grain with gunnysacks to the stone mill. Some of them sifted, others sift finely, and some built a big pot from clay to put provisions in for the year. With the preparation of the provisions, people also stored salt and peppers, onions, olives, date syrup, and grape syrup for the year. Many Tilkepnaye not only prepared provisions for themselves but also for their relatives in Mosul, Baghdad, and other villages far away. In the 1950s, people sold provisions to merchants, and they carried them to all the villages of Mesopotamia, and from there to other nearby countries, especially after they started hulling in the mill with electricity.

In September, school began (lit., enters). Young children in the first half of the twentieth century wore uniforms: shoqta (a garment like a shirt reaching the feet) and sweaters made at home on the loom, which the people of the house used to operate.

However, after that clothing was bought from the market. Ladies rested from spinning wool thread with the spindle, and also from spinning cotton thread in the spinning wheel, and from the weaving wheel to prepare the spool for weaving. Men rested from preparing thread for weaving in the yard. They rested their legs, their hands, and their ears from the noise of the beam, the shuttle, and the weaving with the loom.

SCHOOLS OF TILKEPE

There was a school for boys in Tilkepe before 1861. The deacon Yousif Ezra opened a school in his house in 1877 in Tilkepe, while other Tilkepnaye opened another school. The two schools were unified in 1889. In 1912, the Reverend Francis Katula took over the administration. The school stopped during the First World War. It was reopened under the administration of Fr. Stephan Qallabat in 1915 and was called the Qasha School. The Cathrinian nuns opened a school in Tilkepe for girls in 1902. After the First World War, the first elementary school for boys was opened under the direction of Fr. Stephan Qallabat in 1919. Tilkepe First Primary School was founded in 1922. In 1946, a second government school, Irfan, opened in Tilkepe.

As for the middle school years for boys, it was in 1949, when the Chaldean Charitable Society in Baghdad inaugurated the Al-Mashreq National School for Boys in St. Joseph Building in Tilkepe, which later became a government school. Later, the preparatory department was added. This school remained a high school during the academic year 1961-1962. In 1956 The Cathrinian nuns opened the elementary school for girls. In 1957, a government primary school for girls opened. By 1959, a government middle school for girls opened. 1962 marked the beginning of co-ed education at St. Joseph's Building at Tilkepe High School.

VOWELS ܙܵܘܥܹܐ

The Aramaic language has seven vowels. These are listed below with their names and examples.

The Seven Aramaic Vowels ܙܵܘܥܹܐ: ܫܲܒ݂ܥܵܐ: ܩܵܕ݂ܘܵܝܹܐ

	Vowel Name		Sound		Example	
1	ܙܩܵܦ݂ܵܐ	݂	long a	aa	ܡܵ	ܡܵܪܝܵܐ	Lord
2	ܦܬ݂ܵܚܵܐ	݂	short a	ah	ܡܲ	ܡܲܠܟܵܐ	King
3	ܘܟ݂ܵܙܵܐ ܟ݂ܸܣܝܵܐ	݂	short i	i	ܡܸ	ܡܸܫܚܵܐ	Oil
4	ܘܟ݂ܵܙܵܐ ܝܸܥܝܵܐ	݂	long ay	ay	ܪܹ	ܪܹܫܵܐ	Head
5	ܙܩܵܦ݂ܵܐ	ܿ	long o	oh	ܿ	ܢܚܝܪܵܐ	Nose
6	ܪܒ݂ܵܨܵܐ	ܘ	long ou	ou	ܘ	ܙܘܙܹܐ	Money
7	ܚܒ݂ܵܨܵܐ	݂	long ee	ee	݂	ܡܫܝܚܵܐ	Christ

41

Chapter 11
THE EVENTS OF OCTOBER

In these days, the sky of Tilkepe was filled with many varieties of birds: skylarks, finches, starlings, hedge sparrows, and then the mountain birds, such as quail, wild pigeons, and doves. Fowlers, at this time, would wait to take their traps out of the crawlspace. If the traps were old and useless, they threw them away and replaced them with new traps. Every fowler looks at the traps one by one. He puts them around the trap tester. He prepares the wooden catch from strong wood, and the peg is hit into the ground, and the thread of cotton, and then moist, new grain. Then he makes a hole in them, and he puts the thread in those grains, which are prepared for the trap.

The fowler of Tilkepe arises early in the morning, before the bird awakens. When he reaches the field, he makes a place for the trap with his hatchet. He covers the trap, and does not allow himself to be seen, only the grain. Then he smooths it with dust around the grain. He places three clods of dirt: one on the right side, another on the left, and the other on the head of the trap. Then the fowler waits for the light of the sky.

When the flock of birds starts moving, he begins praying that maybe they will land on the ground where his traps are. Sometimes he himself chases them from neighboring places to move them toward his traps. Some fowlers used to trap between ten and fifty quails or wild pigeons or doves in one day. Some used to catch between one hundred to two hundred skylarks, finches, or starlings. Some of the fowlers used to take skewers with them and barbecued in the field. In the evening when the fowlers returned, their own little children welcomed them to take from them starlings, and they held the starlings by their wings and made them sing.

When the fowler entered the house, all the people of the household came around him to pluck the birds and to barbecue or fry them, and put the birds' heads over the charcoal in the manqal or in the hot dish with gurgur or pearled barley. They sold the feathers to people, and those people put them in their pillows. They cleaned skylarks, or the rest of the birds, and sold them in the morning in the market. Not only fowlers caught birds, but also people with hounds would go to the field searching for rabbits and deer for their meat, and foxes for their skin.

On foggy days (lit., "in the day of fog") some people would search around the telephone wires of the pipe of water, and they would catch birds with broken wings. And there were some others who went fishing in places which had water, especially in the Tigris River or in Benedawaya (near Alqosh) or in the Khawessra River or in the other rivers around the villages of the Chaldeans of Nineveh.

THE COW IS A BLESSING IN THE HOUSE

Every household in the villages of Nineveh had at least one cow. From the early morning, they sent the cow to the cattle area. In the evening, it came back alone and loaded with milk. They milked it and warmed the milk. When they poured milk into the cooking pot, the small children fought over the milk residue. They put yeast in the milk, and the next day it would become yogurt. They produced cheese from the milk. The curds of the yogurt were kept only for the older workers of the household., After shaking the yogurt, they made butter for cooking and mayana (liquid) or kishya (thick) or khamusa (sour) yogurt.

The yogurt of autumn was more delicious than the rest of the year because those who made yogurt in the summer produced khamusa (sour), and in the winter, they produced mayana (liquid); but in the fall, the weather was not too hot nor too cold. The yogurt leavened well, and they said, "From the yogurt of the fall, a sister does not feed her sister with it" (i.e., because it is so good).

Some people in Tilkepe kept sheep, and from the milk of the sheep, they made yogurt or cheese. Many in these days kept cattle for slaughter, either lambs or calves, and they slaughtered them the week of Christmas or Easter. Before electricity entered the villages, some people slaughtered those kept animals: calves, bulls, or lambs. They brought water, put salt in it, and to know that there is enough salt they floated an egg in the saltwater. If it floated, they poured the salt water in the crock, and they put pieces of meat in it. They covered the mouth of that crock or pot. They buried it in a cold place in the basements. They also did it this way when they wanted to keep cheese and olives for an entire year. From those they ate all winter.

Chapter 12
THE EVENTS OF NOVEMBER
FACTORIES OF TAHINI IN TILKEPE

Strong and cold wind strike from all sides in this month. The makers of tahini prepare their mills. They bring sesame from the mountain (north). They soak them, and then hull them in the stone wheel. They take off their shell with another tool called makhidhranuneh (a large round stone). Then they winnow them and spread them out to dry. Then they fry them and throw them in the mill. Finally, they make tahini from them. There was no area without one or two mills. Neighbors and strangers carried their own pans with them to buy waqiyat (a measurement) of tahini. Some also bought kuspa (thick sesame seeds) or shireq (sesame oil) for cooking and frying instead of oil. Tahini and date syrup or grape syrup were the daily food for many poor people.

OUZO (ARAK), WINE AND VINEGAR FACTORIES

Dates and raisins in these days were readily available in Tilkepe. Many people not only ate dates and raisins but also heated them and squeezed them to make Ouzo, wine, and vinegar. The odor of pure ouzo with mistakkeh (black licorice herb) spread in the alleys of the village.

Weak arak, which makes people drunk but does not make the head dizzy, was made out of dates. However, the dry and strong arak made people dizzy and served hot was delicious. They made it out of grapes.

This is how they made distilled arak in the house: They brought dates or raisins and they put them in a large pot filled with water. They waited forty days, but every week one of the household members came, stirred, and mixed the moist raisins with a large wooden spoon. At the end of forty days, they moved the raisins to another large pot. They put a cover on this pot and sealed it with mud on all sides. They left a place for a reed made into a long tube, which went to another pot. They burned fire under the pot, which had the moistened dates or raisins. The vapor, which came out from the first pot, went through the tube and started to drip droplets into the second, cold pot. Before they put fire under the first pot, they put in it sparigleh and mistakkeh (both licorice herbs) and apples, and the meat of the rooster or the hen. All things moistened together in the pot and the good smell of arak made the workers forget their hard work and effort and the work of fifty days.

A long time ago, when there was a wedding in the family, the arak was very abundant, and put in small, wide ceramic jars or water vases or in the pot. Everybody, the relatives or the friends, was able to drink or to fill a bottle or have a bottle or a flask. When they paraded in the village, and when the wedding party passed before the house of the friends, the people of that house stood before the door and they offered a flask, first for the groom and the bride and then the people of the parade, young and old.

Inside of Youth Bible Study Group (Circa 1965)

We put our hope in God   As well as in the Virgin Mary
To intercede from her son Our Lord Jesus
so that Tilkepe may prosper and grow

Imoodan b-alaha eeleh derya   Wmart Mariam ayeh denmanyah
Min bronah Eshoa Marya   D-Tilkepe roya w-farya

APPENDIX
TILKEPE IS AMONG THE MOST WELL-KNOWN CHRISTIAN VILLAGES IN IRAQ

The Iraqi Department of Antiquities conducted an excavation in Tilkepe of its antiquities and found pottery dating back to the second millennium B.C. From the findings of this excavation, the hypothesis could be formed that links Tilkepe as a northern suburb of Nineveh from the time of the mighty Nimrod who founded the city of Nineveh, mentioned in Genesis 10:10. History shows that the hill which Tilkepe was built on in 705-681 B.C. was used as a fortress to protect Nineveh.

In the year 1868, Tilkepnaye discovered a well while burying elders at the top of the hill. At the bottom of the well, there was a wide cave containing clear water. (See p. 3-4 in Tilkepe by Bazzi, for the full story). At the beginning of the fourth century B.C., Tilkepe was mentioned by the Greek leader Xenophon when he passed by it with his army.

Tilkepe includes 26 Khirbet or building ruins. Tilkepe lands are divided into 23 districts. Its area is 36 and 924 thousand dunums. (A dunum in Iraq was a Turkish measurement of land area enclosing 2,500 square meters). The agricultural lands contain 88 square kilometers, surrounded by Batnaya from the north, from the south by Baouira and Rashidiya, from the east, the Khosar River and the lands of Bashiqa, and from the west, Wana.

When Christianity spread, the Chaldeans guided Mesopotamia with the preaching of St. Thomas the Apostle, Mar Addy, and Mar Mary from the first century A.D. The people of Tilkepe converted to Christianity and joined the Chaldean Church, which embraced and preached the Catholic faith until the beginning of the sixth century

A.D., when the Chaldean Church departed from Rome and in 1552, it reunited with it again.

The Catholic faith began in Tilkepe in 1617, if not before. Little by little, it penetrated until the second decade of the nineteenth century, when the rest of Tilkepnaye joined the Catholic faith, practiced Catholicism and still are Catholic.

Tilkepe is famous for the presence of the monastery of St. Kirakoson on the south side of the hill. Even medieval historians have called it the village built alongside the Monastery of Mar Quriaqos. Sacred Heart Church is built over the ruins of the monastery.

The Tilkepnaye, with other Christians of Mesopotamia, from the time of Jesus until today, were persecuted by Gentiles who were not of their religion. The Gentiles killed thousands upon thousands of Christians and destroyed monasteries and churches. Christians were subject to massacres, which led to a significant decrease in their numbers, especially by the Tatar in 1253, the Kurds in 1286, and Tamerlane in 1400. The Mongols conquered Tilkepe twice: in 1508 and then 1562. Nadarshah conquered Tilkepe in 1743. In 1838 Tilkepe was conquered by Mirakur, the ruler of Rawandus.

In September 1970, the Archdiocese of Mosul was assigned to Father Ibrahim Ibrahim (now the Bishop) to open a Seminary in Tilkepe. A small group of students, comprising students from the dioceses of the North, attended the seminary. The project lasted four years. The first two years were under the administration of Father Ibrahim. In addition, the last two years were managed by Father Naguib Gago.

Catechism Class for Tilkepe Youth (Circa 1960)

الْحِكَــمُ مُتِّجِّدِ (ܝܘܿܡܳܝܳܬ݂ܳܐ) ܘܚܘܼܕ݂ܪ̈ܶܐ

Daily wisdoms - Wise sayings

1. The foundation of wisdom is the fear of God.
(راس الحكمة مخافة الله) ܪܺܫܳܐ ܕ݂ܚܶܟ݂ܡܬ݂ܳܐ: ܘܕ݂ܶܚܠܬ݂ܳܐ ܟܝܶܐ ܡܶܢ݂ܟܶܬ݂ܳܐ:

2. People who live in glass houses should not throw stones on others.
(الذي بيته من الزجاج لا يلقي الحجارة على الآخرين)
ܗܘ ܕ݂ܒܰܝܬ݂ܶܗ ܒܓ݂ܳܓ݂ܶ ܡܶܢ ܣܘܼܡܕ݂ܰܢܟ݂ܳܐ: ܠܐ ܦ݂ܰܝܢܶܐ ܟܺܐܦ݂ܶܐ ܚܶܢܩ݂ܶܐ:

3. The eye does not satisfy from watching, nor the ear from listening.
(لا تشبع العين من النظر ولا الأذن من السماع) ܠܐ ܚܰܝܳܒܳܐ ܒܰܝܢܳܐ ܡܶܢ ܚܶܢܩ݂ܳܐ: ܘܠܐ ܢܶܐܩ݂ܳܐ ܡܶܢ ܥܶܒ݂ܕ݂ܳܐ

4. Whoever sows the thorns should not walk barefoot.
(من يزرع الشوك عليه أن لا يسير حافيا) ܗܘ ܕ݂ܙܳܪܶܥ ܓܶܡܛ݂ܶܐ: ܠܐ ܢܙ݂ܶܝܚ ܦ݂ܰܚܩ݂ܰܢܳܐ

5. Whoever digs the well for people will fall in it.
(من يحفر البئر لغيره هو الذي يقع فيها) ܗܘ ܕ݂ܚܳܪܶܕ ܒܶܐܪ݂ܳܐ ܗܶܐ ܗܰܘ ܗܶܢܬ݂ܶܐ: ܢܳܘܶܐܘ ܚܢܶܝܕ݂ ܚܢܟ݂ܳܘܶܐ

6. Love and talk; hate and talk.
(حب واحكي أبغض واحكي) ܚܶܒ ܘܡܳܣܚܶܪ: ܣܶܒ ܘܡܳܣܚܶܪ

7. Whoever sows the wind will reap the whirlwind.
(من يزرع الريح يحصد العاصفة) ܗܘ ܕ݂ܙܳܪܶܥ ܦ݂ܰܚܘܶܐ: ܚܢܶܝܕ ܒܰܝܠܝܶܐ

8. If you do not have what you want, want what you have.
(اذا لا يكن ما تريد رد ما يكون) ܝܺܢ ܠܐ ܦ݂ܰܝܢܶܐ ܠܰܝܒܶܝܕ ܒܰܚܒܺܝܟ݂ܰܝܶܐ: ܟ݂ܝܶܐܡ ܚܶܒܺܝܒܶܕ ܒܰܝܗܘܘܶܢ

9. With the fire of the evil ones, the good ones are burned.
(بنار الأشرار يحترق المساكين) ܢܘܼܪ݂ܳܐ ܕ݂ܒ݂ܺܝܫܶܐ: ܚܒܺܝܚܕ ܡܶܗܓܝܶܬ݂ܶܐ

10. The lowland brings better harvest.
(الأرض المنخفضة تعطي زرعا صالحا) ܐܶܕ݂ܳܐ ܣ݂ܰܗܒܝܶܐ: ܚܶܒܘܼܢܶܐ ܘܶܕ݂ܳܐ ܦ݂ܰܝܬ݂ܳܐ

11. A person cannot give more than he has.
(الإنسان لا يمكنه أن يعطي اكثر مما عنده) ܢܰܝܬ݂ܳܐ ܠܒܰܝܗ ܒܰܝܗ݂ܰܥܒܶܕ: ܝܥܶܚܬ݂ܝܶܐ ܡܶܢ ܡܳܐ ܕ݂ܒ݂ܺܝܬ݂ܶܗ

12. Paradise without people would not be enjoyable.
(الفردوس من دون البشر ليس ممتعا) ܦ݂ܰܕ݂ܘܼܣܶܐ ܕ݂ܠܐ ܢܰܝܬ݂ܳܐ: ܠܰܝܠ݂ܶܐ ܒܰܗܒܺܝܬ݂ܳܐ

13. Tell me who your friends are, and I will tell you who you are.

(قل لي من هو صديقك لأقول لك من أنتَ) ܐܝܡܢܐܠܝ ܡܢܘ ܚܒܪܘܟ ܦܬܚܒܪܘܟ: ܘܒܝܡܢܘܟ ܡܢܘ ܐܝܬܘܟ

14. The Lord Gives, the Lord Takes, blessed be His name.

(الله يعطي والله يأخذ لكن ليكن اسمه مباركا) ܡܪܝܐ ܝܗܒ ܘܡܪܝܐ ܢܣܒ: ܗܘܐ ܫܡܗ ܡܒܘܪܟܐ

15. When the cat is away the mice will play.

(حينما يغيب القط تلعب الفئران) ܐܝܡܢ ܦܝܫܐ ܓܝܪ ܗܟܘܬܐ ܩܛܢܐ: ܥܟܘܪܐ ܡܫܥܒܒܝ ܘܡܫܬܥܝܢ

16. If God does not build the house, the effort of the builders is in vain.

(اذا الرب لا يبني البيت. عبثا يتعب البناؤون) ܐܢ ܡܪܝܐ ܠܐ ܒܢܐ ܒܝܬܐ: ܣܪܝܩܐ ܥܡܠܝ ܕܒܢܝܐ

17. A monkey in the eye of his mother is a deer.

(القرد بعين امه غزال) ܩܘܦܐ ܒܥܝܢܐ ܕܐܡܗ ܕܝܙܐ: ܓܙܠܐ ܝܠܗ

18. Some would strain off the gnat and swallow the camel.

(هناك من يبلعون الجَمَل لكن يصفّون البَق) ܐܝܬ ܕܒܠܥ ܓܡܠܐ ܡܨܠܠܐ: ܘܡܨܠܝ ܓܢܨܐ

19. Every human being, will be judged by God, according to his deeds.

(كل شخص يدينه الله حسب أعماله) ܟܠ ܒܪܢܫܐ: ܐܠܗܐ ܕܐܝܢܠܗ ܐܝܟ ܥܒܕܘܗܝ

20. Close the door that brings the draft, and then relax.

(الباب الذي يأتيك منه الريح سده واستريح) ܬܪܥܐ ܕܐܬܝܐ ܡܢܗ ܦܘܚܐ ܣܟܘܪ ܗܝܕܝܟ ܘܢܘܚ

21. The head that is not peaceful is not blessed.

(الراس المضطرب لا يكن مباركا) ܪܝܫܐ ܕܠܐ ܗܘܐ ܡܒܝܢܐ: ܠܐ ܗܘܐ ܡܒܘܪܟܐ

22. Whenever a poor man has something, he is often asked, "Where did it come from?" However, the rich man is congratulated for what he has.

(الفقير من أين لك؟ والغني مبارك لك) ܡܣܟܢܐ ܡܢ ܐܝܟܐ ܐܬܝܠܘܟ ؟ ܘܥܬܝܪܐ ܡܒܘܪܟܐ ܠܟܘܟ

23. An Idle mind is the devil's workshop.

(رأس الإنسان البطّال دكان للشيطان) ܪܝܫܐ ܕܒܪܢܫܐ ܒܛܝܠܐ: ܕܘܟܢܐ ܕܝܠܗ ܕܣܛܢܐ

24. A close neighbor is better than a brother who lives away.

(الجار القريب خير من الأخ البعيد) ܫܒܒܐ ܩܘܪܒܐ: ܛܒܗ ܐܝܠܗ ܡܢ ܐܚܘܢܐ ܪܚܘܩܐ

25. God provides food for the birds, but He does not put the food in their nest.

(الله يهيئ الطعام للطيور لكنه لا يضعه في عشّها)

ܐܠܗܐ ܡܬܩܢ ܡܐܟܘܠܬܐ ܗܐ ܠܦܪܚܐ: ܐܠܝ ܠܐ ܡܬܘܗܠܐ ܓܘ ܩܢܗ

26. When the blind lead the blind, both fall into the ditch.

(لما الأعمى يقود الأعمى كلاهما يقعان في الحفرة)

ܝ݉ ܗܡܢܐ ܠܗܡܢܐ ܡܕܒܪ: ܗ݉ܬܪ݉ܘܗܝܢ݉ܝ݉ ܬܪ݉ܒܩܠܒ ܬܪ݉ܗܘܡ݉ܬܐ

27. Cry, and you will cry alone; laugh, and the whole world laughs with you.

(ابكي تبكي وحدك اضحك يضحك كل الناس معك)

ܬܒܪ ܬܬܚܝܗ ܠܢܦܘܕܘܗ : ܚܢܦܗ ܚܠ݉ܟ ܢ݉ܬ݉ܬܐ ܬܠ݉ܢܝܚܒ ܝ݉ܗܡܗ

28. When the mouth eats, the eye returns the favor.

(يأكل الفم وتستحي العيون)   ܢ݉ܝܟܠ ܝ݉ܦܡܐ: ܘܚܢ݉ܒܓܒ ܠ݉ܢ݉ܬ݉ܐ

29. The nest of the crane that is blind, is built by God.

(عشّ اللقلق الأعمى يبنيه الله)   ܣ݉ܘܝܗ ܝ݉ܟܠܟܠܝ݉ܕ ܗܡܢܐ: ܝ݉ܠ݉ܗ݉ܐ ܚ݉ܬܝ݉ܒ݉ܗ

30. Out of sight, out of mind.

(ما هو أمام العين ليس أمام القلب)   ܡ݉ܝ݉ܓܝ݉ ܝ݉ܟ݉ܝ݉ܠܝܗ ܬ݉ܬ݉ܡ݉ܝ݉ܢ ܝ݉ܟ݉ܒ݉ܬ݉ܢ: ܗ݉ܡ ܬ݉ܬ݉ܡ݉ܝ݉ܢ ܝ݉ܟ݉ܬ݉ܢ ܟ݉ܝ݉ܠ݉ܝܗ

31. Do not swear, do not ask others to swear, and do not stand behind the one who swears.

(لا تحلف ولا تجعل الآخر يحلف ولا تقف خلف من يحلف)

ܠ݉ܐ ܬ݉ܢܝ݉ܗ: ܘܠ݉ܐ ܗܘ݉ܡ݉ܝ݉ܗ: ܘܠ݉ܐ ܬ݉ܝ݉ܘܕ ܝ݉ܬ݉ܢ݉ܬ ܒ݉ܢ݉ܥ݉ܠ݉ܗ

32. The one who is full does not feel the stomach of the one who is hungry.

(الشبعان لا يشعر ببطن الجائع)   ܗ݉ܒ݉ܝ݉ܟ݉ܢ ܠ݉ܐ ܚ݉ܕ݉ܝ݉ܥ ܬ݉ܚ݉ܕ݉ܦ݉ܢ ܝ݉ܚ݉ܩ݉ܒ݉ܢܐ

33. One's stomach may be full, but his eye is hungry.

(البطن مليئة لكن العين جائعة)   ܟ݉ܦ݉ܢ ܗ݉ܝ݉ܕ݉ܟ݉ܡ݉ܐ: ܘܝ݉ܢ݉ܬ݉ܢ ܚ݉ܩ݉ܝ݉ܒ݉ܡ݉ܝ

34. Do not open a door that you cannot close.

(لا تفتح الباب الذي لا يمكنك غلقه)   ܠ݉ܐ ܦ݉ܬ݉ܚ݉ܝܗ ܗ݉ܕ݉ܬ݉ܢ: ܝ݉ܠ݉ܝ݉ܬ݉ܘܗ ܝ݉ܬ݉ܠ݉ܩ݉ܝ݉ܗ

35. Each person will be rewarded, according to his deeds.

(كل إنسان. مثل عمله تكون مكافأته)   ܚ݉ܠ݉ ܢ݉ܢ݉ܬ݉ܢ: ܡ݉ܝ݉ܕ݉ܝ݉ ܗ݉ܘ݉ܟ݉ܬ݉ܝ݉ܗ ܝ݉ܝ݉ܘܗ݉ܘܗ ܗ݉ܘܕ݉ܚ݉ܝ݉ܗ

36. A tree is known by its fruit.

(الشجرة من ثمارها تُعرف)   ܝ݉ܠ݉ܢ݉ܬ݉ܢ ܡ݉ܢ ܝ݉ܕ݉ܩ݉ܗ ܚ݉ܩ݉ܝ݉ܬ݉ܢ ܝ݉ܝ݉ܕ݉ܝ݉ܟ݉ܝ݉ܗ

37. The way you measure others is the way you will be measured and more.

(بالكيل الذي به تكيل لك ويُزاد)   ܬ݉ܟ݉ܢ݉ܟ݉ ܝ݉ܝ݉ܟ݉ܝܗ: ܬ݉ܩ݉ܝ݉ܒ ܚ݉ܒ݉ܟ݉ ܝ݉ܟ݉ܠ݉ܝ݉ܘܗ ܘܗ݉ܘܘܒ݉ܝ݉ܕ

38. Whatever a person plants, will be harvested.

(ما يزرعه الإنسان إياه يحصد)   ܡܸܢܕܝ ܕܙܵܪܥ ܒܲܪܢܵܫܵܐ: ܠܵܗܹܗ ܚܵܨܹܕ

39. Do unto others as you want them to do unto you.

(إعمل مع الآخرين كما تريد أن يعمل معك الآخرون)

ܥܒܘܼܕ ܥܲܡ ܕܝܼܢܹܐ: ܐܲܝܟܲ ܕܚܵܒܹܬ ܕܥܵܒܕܝܼ ܥܲܡܘܼܟܲ ܫܲܪܟܵܐ

40. Listen, but speak little.

(اسمع كثيرا وتكلّم قليلا)   ܫܡܘܼܥ ܓܘܼܒܵܐ ܘܡܲܠܸܠ ܒܝܼܙ

41. The person who spent his time sleeping on his side, will starve to death.

(من يبقى نائما على جنبه يموت من جوعه)   ܐܵܘ ܕܦܵܐܸܫ ܕܡܝܼܟܵܐ ܠܘܼܟܬܹܗ: ܚܵܫܹܚ ܡܲܝܸܬ

42. Hell is full of those who think evil

(الجحيم مليئة من الظانين)   ܓܗܲܢܵܐ: ܡܠܝܼܬܵܐ ܡܠܵܒܹ̈ܐ ܓܲܒ ܒܝܼܫܵܐ

43. Whoever sows in tears, will harvest in joy.

(من يزرع بالدموع يحصد بالفرح)   ܐܵܘ ܕܙܵܪܹܥ ܒܕܸܡܥ̈ܐ: ܚܵܨܹܕ ܒܚܲܕܘܼܬ̈ܐ

44. Stretch your leg according to your blanket.

(مُد رجلك على قدر لحافك)   ܦܫܘܼܛ ܐܸܩܠܘܼܟ: ܠܲܝܟܵܐ ܕܝܼܠܵܟ

45. Be shrewd as serpents and simple as doves.

(كونوا حكماء كالحياة ودعاء كالحمام)   ܗܘܹܐ ܦܲܪܥܝܼܕ̈ ܐܲܝܟܲ ܚܘܵܘ̈ܬܵܐ: ܘܦܫܝܼܛܐ ܐܲܝܟܲ ܝܵܘܢ̈ܐ

46. Do not get wet before it rains.

(لا تتبلل قبل أن يأتي المطر)   ܠܵܐ ܬܵܪܹܐ ܡܲܢ ܩܲܕܸܡ ܕܐܵܬܹܐ ܡܸܛܪܵܐ

47. The eye, which did not see, avoids doing wrong.

(العين التي لم ترَ لم تُخطئ)   ܥܲܝܢܵܐ ܕܠܵܐ ܚܙܝܼܬܵܐ: ܠܵܐ ܣܝܼܢܟܵܐ

48. A bird in your hand is better than having ten in the tree.

(عصفور في اليد خير من عشرة فوق الشجر)   ܨܸܦܪܵܐ ܓܲܒ ܐܝܼܕܘܼܟ ܝܵܠܵܗ ܥܒܝܼܕܵܐ ܡܲܢ ܝܲܨܪܵܐ ܠܐܝܼܠܵܢܵܐ

49. Close the door on yesterday and tomorrow, enjoy today.

(اغلق الباب على البارحة والغد وتمتع بنهارك)   ܕܠܘܼܩ ܬܲܪܥܵܐ ܠܬܸܡܵܠ ܘܡܲܚܪܢܵܐ: ܘܚܲܕܹܐ ܠܝܵܘܡܘܟ

50. Whoever keeps a grudge in his heart holds a snake in his chest.

(من حَمَلَ ضغينة في قلبه حمل ثعباناً في صدره)   ܐܵܘ ܕܛܵܥܸܢ ܚܸܡܬܵܐ ܠܸܒܹܗ: ܚܙܝܼܪܹܗ ܫܲܝܕܵܐ (ܚܵܘܕܲܢܵܐ) ܚܲܝܵܐ

51

ملاحظة أولى: إن المرحوم زريف جابرو قد ألّف قصائد وأشعار شعبية يغنيها تلكيبنايه في أفراحهم. إنني انقل مع التنقيح الشخصي قصيدتين:

١- بعض الأبيات من باقله .   ٢- بين كالو وخماثا .

ملاحظة ثانية: ربما يوجد من لا تعجبه بعض التغييرات التي وضعتُها لأنها تختلف قليلا عن الشعر الأصلي. لكن حينما بدأتُ بترجمتها، كان من المستحيل إبقاء بعض التعابير مثلا (بشَرّه وباباي عويله!).

ملاحظة ثالثة: اشكر الشماس سلام بطي والإخوة الذين ساعدوني لأجمع هذه القصائد التي هي مبعثرة إلا في ذاكرة البعض.

قصيــدة الباقـــلاء ܦܘܐܬܐ ܕܒܩܝܠܐ. Poem on beans

ܡܐ ܛܥܡܝܗ ܒܩܝܠܐ (٢)   ܟܠ ܡܝܕܝ ܕܒܩܝܠܐ (٢)

الــردة: ما اطيب الباقلاء (٢)   كل ما يحدث لي هو بسبب الباقلاء (٢)

How delicious are the beans (2) all that happens to me is because of the beans (2)

١- ܘܙܒܢܝ ܒܐܪܥܐ ܛܠܝܬܢܐ:ܒܓܘܒܗ̇ ܡܬܐ ܕܡܕܢܚܢܐ:ܦܠܝܚܝܗ ܚܓܝܒܐ ܕܦܕܢܐ: ܘܟܠܗ ܘܐܡܠܐ ܒܩܝܠܐ٭

ܡܐ ܛܥܡܝܗ ܒܩܝܠܐ (٢)   ܟܠ ܡܝܕܝ ܕܒܩܝܠܐ (٢)

اشتريت أرضا صالحة: قريبة من الجهة الشرقية: محروثة بسكة الفدان كلها مزروعة باقلاء.

الــردة : ما اطيب الباقلاء (٢)   كل ما يحدث لي هو بسبب الباقلاء (٢)

I bought a good land near by the East side. Plowed by the farmer, all planted with beans.
How delicious are the beans (2) all that happens to me is because of the beans (2)

٢- ܘܙܒܢܝ ܒܗܝܟܠܐ ܡܢܛܪܢ:ܡܬܐ ܕܓܡܕܝܗ ܒܝܟܒܗ: ܕܩܝ ܘܣܬܝܒܝ ܟܘܟܬܝܗ: ܘܚܕܥܒ ܡܝܢܗ ܟܕ ܓܝܗ:
ܓܗ ܒܕ ܚܘܕܢܗܕ ܒܩܝܠܐ٭

ܘܟܠܗ ܡܝܕܝܗ ܕܒܩܝܠܐ (٢)   ܘܡܐ ܛܥܡܝܗ ܒܩܝܠܐ (٢)

اشتريت رطلا من الباقلاء من النوع الذي تعرفه. حُبوبُه كبيرة وممتلئة: وابني لم يأكل منها إلّا جرّة من الباقلاء.

الـــردّة: ما اطيب الباقلاء (٢)   كل ما يحدث لي هو بسبب الباقلاء (٢)

I bought a pound of beans of the kind you know. Bean large and full. My son did not eat but only a jar of it.

How delicious are the beans (2) all that happens to me is because of the beans (2)

في منتصف الليل انزعجتُ وصرخت إلى والدي ليساعدني. اجلب لي طبيبا من الموصل لكي أتخلص من مرضي.

الـــردة : ما اطيب الباقلاء (٢)   كل ما يحدث لي هو بسبب الباقلاء (٢)

In the middle of the night, I was upset and asked my father to help me: Bring a doctor from Mosul to get rid of my illness.

How delicious are the beans (2) all that happens to me is because of the beans (2)

جاء الطبيب المشهور وأخذ يفحص بطني. شفيتُ حالا فاستغرب الطبيب وقال إن الألم الذي كان لك قد زال. كل ما حدث بسبب أكلك الباقلاء.

الـــردة : ما اطيب الباقلاء (٢)   كل ما يحدث لي هو بسبب الباقلاء (٢)

A famous doctor came and started examining my stomach. I soon recovered, so the doctor was surprised and said, "Your pain is over. Everything that happened to you, due to eating the beans.

How delicious are the beans (2) all that happens to me is because of the beans (2)

A Folk Song from Tilkepe
Between Mother-in-law and Daughter-in-law
ܙܡܘܪܬܐ ܡܢ ܬܠܟܐܦܐ: ܒܝܢܬ ܟܠܘ ܘܚܡܬܐ

(1)	(1)	(ܐ)
Between the mother-in-law and the daughter-in-law;	Baynath kaloo wikhmatha	ܒܝܢܬ ܟܠܘ ܘܚܡܬܐ
Come and see what is going on.	Hawar mah brayleh	ܗܘܪ ܡܐ ܒܪܝܠܗ
Today and for the past two days,	Edyoo tre yomatha	ܐܕܝܘ ܬܪܐ ܝܘܡܬܐ
They have been fighting. Even their dog started to bark.	Bsharre wkalbayih a-wayle	ܒܫܪܐ ܘܟܠܒܝܗ ܥܘܝܠܗ
The groom is stuck in the middle of them.	Oh gawra hmeela b-palga	ܐܘ ܓܒܪܐ ܚܡܝܠܐ ܒܦܠܓܐ
He tries to reconcile them, but his heart is broken.	Msalohe wlibbeh dwayleh	ܡܨܠܘܚܐ ܘܠܒܗ ܕܘܝܠܗ
So, he silenced his own family.	Ta dmaskin nashe diyeh	ܬܐ ܕܡܫܟܢ ܢܫܐ ܕܝܗ
He ran away like a crazy man.	Ireqle w-hijleh b-alole	ܥܪܩܠܗ ܘܗܝܓܠܗ ܒܥܠܘܠܐ

بين الكنّة والحماة انظروا ماذا حدث اليوم هو الثاني وهما تتشاجران وكلبهما ينبح. الزوج واقف في الوسط يصالحهما، حتى ذاب قلبه لكي يُسكِت أهله، هرب وهاج في الشوارع.

(2)	(2)	(ܒ)
The mother-in-law said, "Hey everybody!	Khmatha mayrah ya nashe	ܚܡܵܬܵܗ ܡܝܼܪܵܗ ܝܵܐ ܐ�̃ܢܵܫܹܐ
What kind of unloved daughter-in-law do I have?	Ma kaloo itty sneetha	ܡܵܐ ܟܲܠܘܼ ܕܒܸܟܒܝܼ ܣܢܝܼܬܵܐ
If I wasn't there,	Ella hoyanwa ana	ܐܸܠܵܐ ܗܘܹܝܵܢܘܵܐ ܐܵܢܵܐ
her husband would abuse her every day.	Koodiom Igawrah mkheetha	ܟܘܼܕܝܼܘܿܡ ܠܓܲܒܪܵܗ ܡܚܝܼܬܵܐ
I'm done with her, she's lazy.	Bassy minnah Kislani	ܒܲܣܝ ܡܸܢܵܗ ܟܸܣܠܵܢܝ
She doesn't even turn down the beds.	Laybah ta dparsa shweetha	ܠܹܝܒܵܗ ܗܵܐ ܕܦܵܪܣܵܐ ܫܘܝܼܬܵܐ
What should I do? Where should I run?	Mah odan w-aika zaly	ܡܵܐ ܥܘܿܕܝ ܘܐܲܝܟܵܐ ܙܵܠܝ
This is something that has never occurred and never happened."	La breethala w-la hweetha	ܠܵܐ ܒܪܝܼܬܵܠܵܗ ܐܵܦܠܵܐ ܘܠܵܐ ܗܘܝܼܬܵܐ

قالت الحماة يا ناس عندي كنة مكروهة. لو لم أكن أنا، لكانت كل يوم مضروبة من زوجها. تعبتُ منها هذه الكسلانة، إنها حتى لا تفرش الفراش. ماذا أعمل وإلى أين اذهب. مثل هذا الأمر لم يحدث أبدا.

(3)	(3)	(ܓ)
The daughter-in-law said, "She is lying!	Kaloo mayrah mdooglaylah	ܟܲܠܘܼ ܡܝܼܪܵܗ ܡܕܘܿܓܠܲܝܠܵܗ
This old woman is filled with fleas.	Sotoo mleetha pertayne	ܣܵܬܘܿ ܡܠܝܼܬܵܐ ܦܸܪ̈ܬܲܝܢܹܐ
My husband will not trade me.	Gawry la kimbadilly	ܓܲܒܪܝ ܠܵܐ ܟܡܒܲܕܸܠܝ
I mean more to him than roses and lilies.	La bwarde wla b-reehane	ܠܵܐ ܒܘܲܪ̈ܕܹܐ ܐܵܦܠܵܐ ܒܪ̈ܝܼܚܵܢܹܐ
If I catch my mother-in-law,	In ta-asa khmathy b-eedy	ܐܹܢ ܛܲܥܣܵܐ ܚܡܵܬܝ ܒܐܝܼܕܝ
I will make her disappear like smoke.	B-fanyanah mikh tnane	ܒܦܲܢܝܵܢܵܗ ܡܸܟ݂ ܬܢܵܢܹܐ
I will put yoke on her neck,	W-neera bdarian l-paqartah	ܘܢܝܼܪܵܐ ܒܕܵܪܝܵܢ ܠܦܲܩܲܪܬܵܗ

55

In addition, I will make her pull the plow.	W-ptarian bgawah bdanane	ܘܦܛܪܝܢ ܒܓܘܗ ܒܕܢܢܐ

قالت الكنة إن هذه العجوز تكذب. وهي مملوءة من البراغيث. إن زوجي لا يبدّلني لا بالورود ولا بالرياحين. وعندما أراها سوف افنيها مثل الدخان. وسأضع النير على رقبتها وأسوق بها الفدان.

(4)	(4)	(ܕ)
She calls me gluttonous	Kamraly horraneetha	ܟܡܪܠܝ ܚܘܪܢܝܬܐ
While she is laying in her bed.	W-ayih dmikhta bishweetha	ܘܐܝܗ ܕܡܝܟܬܐ ܒܫܘܝܬܐ
With the smell of onions coming from her mouth,	B-ad reekha d-bisla m-kimmah	ܒܐܕ ܪܝܚܐ ܕܒܣܠܐ ܡܟܡܗ
She makes the whole house smell.	Melayleh koolleh baytha	ܡܠܝܠܗ ܟܘܠܗ ܒܝܬܐ
They stuck me with her.	Kim-ma-alqeely bgawah	ܟܝܡܡܥܠܩܝܠܝ ܒܓܘܗ
This old woman is not smart.	Ad sotoo deelah shdeetha	ܐܕ ܣܘܬܘ ܕܝܠܗ ܫܕܝܬܐ
She is spinning the spindle,	Be-a-zala bgo doolaba	ܒܥܙܠܐ ܒܓܘ ܕܘܠܒܐ
I can't get rid of this unbeliever."	Blayly bgawah hanpaytha	ܒܠܝܠܝ ܒܓܘܗ ܚܢܦܝܬܐ

تتهمني بأني شرهة، وهي نائمة في الفراش. ورائحة البصل التي تفوح من فمها ملأت الدار. لقد اجبروني بهذه العجوز الكسول. طوال النهار تغزل بالدولاب. ابتليت بها هذه الغير المؤمنة.

(5)	(5)	(ܗ)
She said, "She is blaming me for spinning the spindle,	Kma-eebali bdoolaba	ܟܡܐܝܒܠܝ ܒܕܘܠܒܐ
But I am lovable!	W-ana d-eewan habbaba	ܘܐܢܐ ܕܐܝܘܢ ܚܒܒܐ
I raised my little boy,	Mdoobary brony zora	ܡܕܘܒܪܝ ܒܪܘܢܝ ܙܥܘܪܐ
Until I made him into a grown man."	Hool d-kim-awdanneh raba	ܗܘܠ ܕܟܝܡܥܘܕܢܗ ܪܒܐ
They stuck me with her.	Kim-ma-alqeeli bgawah	ܟܝܡܡܥܠܩܝܠܝ ܒܓܘܗ

56

She looks like flat, dry manure.	Rabtha w-khishta taptapa	ܪܲܒܬ݂ܵܐ ܘܟ݂ܝܼܫܬܵܐ ܛܲܦܛܲܦܵܐ
Her tongue is one span,	Looshanah eebe seeta	ܠܘܿܫܵܢܵܗ ܐܝܼܒܹܐ ܣܝܼܬܵܐ
And she is not embarrassed or ashamed."	La k-nakhpa w-la ktoraba	ܠܵܐ ܟܢܵܟ݂ܦܵܐ ܘܠܵܐ ܟܬܘܿܪܵܒ݂ܵܐ

تعيّرني بالدولاب وأنا الحبّابة . ربّيت ابني الصغير إلى أن كبر. أجبروني بهذه العجوز التي ابتليت بها،
إنها تشبه الطبطاب. طول لسانها شبر لا تستحي ولا تخجل.

(6)	(6)	(٥)
The bride said, "You people!	Kaloo mayra ya nashe	ܟܲܠܘ ܡܝܼܪܵܐ ܝܵܐ ܢܵܫܹܐ
My heart is done and gone!	Ad libby khlisle w-zille	ܐܵܕ ܠܝܼܒܝ ܟ݂ܠܝܼܣܠܹܐ ܘܙܝܼܠܹܐ
In the morning, she feeds me lentil soup,	M-khooshka k-makhlaly tlawkhe	ܡܢܘܿܫܟܵܐ ܟܡܲܟ݂ܠܵܠܝ ܬܠܵܘܟ݂ܹܐ
and at noon she feeds me fava beans;	W-palga dyoma baqille	ܘܦܲܠܓܵܐ ܕܝܼܘܿܡܵܐ ܒܵܩܝܼܠܹܐ
at night, steamed Swiss chard, and pickled	W-boormashe silqa shleeqa	ܘܒܘܿܪܡܵܫܹܐ ܣܝܼܠܩܵܐ ܫܠܝܼܩܵܐ
Turnip which makes everyone become ill.	W-mkhalaleh milye ay-aylle	ܘܡܟ݂ܲܠܲܠܹܗ ܡܝܼܠܝܹܐ ܐܲܝ ܐܲܝܠܹܐ
This is the way she was raised	Hadakh eelah eelipta	ܗܵܕܲܟ݂ ܐܹܝܠܵܗ ܐܹܝܠܝܼܦܬܵܐ
All the neighbors know about her."	K-yad-ala koolla m-halle	ܟܝܲܕܥܵܠܵܐ ܟܘܿܠܵܐ ܡܗܲܠܹܐ

قالت الكنّة يا ناس قلبي هذا ذاب وانتهى. صباحا تُطعمني العدس وفي الظهر الباقلاء. وفي العشاء السلق
المسلوق والمخلل الخائس. هكذا هي متعلمة يعرفها جميع أفراد المنطقة.

(7)	(7)	(٦)
The mother-in-law said to the daughter-in-law,	Khmatha mayrah ta kaloo	ܚܡܵܬ݂ܵܐ ܡܝܼܪܵܗ ܬܵܐ ܟܲܠܘ
"Away from me, you daughter of beggars!	Ayat brata d-gawooyeh	ܐܲܝܲܬ ܒܪܵܬܵܐ ܕܓܵܘܘܿܝܹܗ

Come and see your dad	Hayo khor bgawid babakh	ܗܲܝܘ ܚܘܿܪ ܒܓܲܘܝܕ ܒܵܒܵܟܼ
Wandering from door to door.	M-tar-aa l-tar-aa mshanoye	ܡܛܲܪܥܵܐ ܠܛܲܪܥܵܐ ܡܫܲܢܘܿܝܹ
Don't you remember	Mo la ka-theewa b-balkh	ܡܘܿ ܠܵܐ ܟܵܬܼܹܐܘܵܐ ܒܒܵܠܟܼ
Your mom begged from me	Yimmakh b-gawi b-nonoyeh	ܝܡܵܟܼ ܒܓܵܘܝ ܒܢܘܿܢܘܿܝܹ
to be my son's wife	Ta d-shaqlanakh ta brony	ܬܵܐ ܕܫܲܩܠܵܢܵܟܼ ܬܵܐ ܒܪܘܿܢܝ
Now you're cursing me over and over.	W-daha l-qara-aa bma-a-woyi	ܘܕܵܗܵܐ ܠܩܲܪܥܵܐ ܒܡܲܥܘܿܝܝ

قالت الحماة للكنة: أنتِ يا ابنة المستجدين. تعالي وانظري إلى والدك وهو ينتقل من باب إلى باب. هلا تذكرين كيف أن امّك كانت تتوسل بي كي أخذك لابني، وأنتِ الآن تسبيني.

(8)	(8)	(ﺡ)
She replied, "Enough! Do not let	Bassa shawqat ta dpalty	ܒܵܣܵܐ ܫܵܘܩܲܬ ܬܵܐ ܕܦܲܠܛܝ
Insults flow from my mouth.	Khabre la rande m-kimmi	ܟܼܵܒܪܹ ܠܵܐ ܪܵܢܕܹ ܡܟܸܡܝ
The mothers of the unmarried,	Koollay yimmatha d-aa-azbe	ܟܘܿܠܲܝ ܝܡܵܬܼܵܐ ܕܐܵܥܲܙܒܹ
Never mentioned anyone else but by name!	La takhreewa ghayr shimmi	ܠܵܐ ܬܵܟܼܪܹܐܘܵܐ ܓܼܲܝܪ ܫܸܡܝ
They used to come to our house	Athawa gayban l-baytha	ܐܵܬܼܵܘܵܐ ܓܲܝܒܲܢ ܠܒܲܝܬܼܵܐ
and beg my mom	M-nonawa bgawid yimmi	ܡܢܘܿܢܵܘܵܐ ܒܓܲܘܝܕ ܝܡܝ
To agree to the promise.	Tad yawawah taneetha	ܬܲܕ ܝܵܘܵܘܲܗ ܬܲܢܝܬܼܵܐ
But my cousin wouldn't allow it."	W-la qabilwa ber d-a-ammi	ܘܠܵܐ ܩܵܒܸܠܘܵܐ ܒܪ ܕܐܲܡܝ

يكفي لا تتركيني أن ألفظ كلمات بذيئة. كل أمهات العزاب لم يذكروا إلا اسمي. كانوا يأتون عندنا إلى البيت. ويتوسلون بأمي حتى ترضى بهم لكن ابن عمي كان يمنع ذلك.

(9)	(9)	(ܛ)
She said, "If your cousin was in love with you,	Bird aa-mmakh n-keebaywalakh	ܒܪ ܕܥܡܡܟܝ ܐܢ ܟܒܝܒܘܠܟܝ
He would have married you!	Bed shaqil walakh taleh	ܒܕܫܩܠ ܗܘܠܟܝ ܬܠܗ
We know he hated you.	K-yadookhwa dsanaywalakh	ܟܝܕܥܘܗܘܐ ܕܣܢܝܘܠܟܝ
You never crossed his mind.	W-har la k-athyatwa b-baleh	ܘܗܪ ܠܐ ܟܐܬܝܬܗܘܐ ܒܒܠܗ
He used to talk about your mistakes	K-mahke ellakh pelmoothakh	ܟܡܚܟܐ ܐܠܟܝ ܦܠܡܘܬܟܝ
To his mother, his sister, and his friends."	Ta yimmeh w-khatheh w-khooreh	ܬܐ ܝܡܗ ܘܚܬܗ ܘܚܒܪܗ
He used to tell people,	W-amirwa oh d-shaqillah	ܘܐܡܪܘܐ ܐܘ ܕܫܩܠܠܗ
"Whoever marries her Will be forever troubled."	B-ma-a-ooya dare d-dareh	ܒܡܥܘܢܐ ܕܪܐ ܕܕܪܗ

ان كان ابن عمك يحبّك لكان قد تزوّجك. لكن جميعنا نعرف بأنه كان يكرهك ولا يفكّر بك. كان يتحدث عن سيئاتك لامه وأخته وأصدقائه. وكان يقول كل من يتزوجها سوف يبتلي بها طول العمر.

(10)	(10)	(ܝ)
She said, "You've said enough!	Bassa a-ad k-malyalakh	ܒܣܐ ܥܕ ܟܡܠܝܠܟܝ
You are stubborn; you never listen.	Ittakh patha d-kthaytha	ܐܝܬܟܝ ܦܬܐ ܕܟܬܝܬܐ
Where would you find another person like me?	Ayka bidkhazyat khwathy	ܐܝܟܐ ܒܕܚܙܝܬ ܟ̰ܘܬܝ
Blushing, white, and beautiful	Smoqta w-khwarta w-khleetha	ܣܡܘܩܬܐ ܘܚܘܪܬܐ ܘܚܠܝܬܐ
I cannot get rid of you.	Kim-ma-ailqeely bgawakh	ܟܡܥܠܩܝܠܝ ܒܓܘܟܝ
You are dark like the ashes from the ash pan!	Komta kh-shimra d-desteetha	ܟܘܡܬܐ ܟ̰ܝ ܫܡܪܐ ܕܕܣܬܝܬܐ
This is what you deserve,	Har hadakh keebatwalakh	ܗܪ ܗܕܟ ܟܒܝܬܗܘܠܟܝ

May you to be forever troubled!"	D-hoyatwa dayim bleetha	ܕܗܘܝܬܘܐ ܕܝܡ ܒܠܝܬܐ

يكفيني من هذا كله إنك جسورة. أين كنت تجدين مثلي حمراء وبيضاء وحلوة. اجبروني بك إنك سوداء مثل رماد الجدرية. هكذا أنت تستحقين أن تكوني طوال عمرك مبتلية.

(11)	(11)	(ܝܐ)
She said, "I don't use rouge or powder,	Hoomra w-pawdir la k-darian	ܣܘܡܩܐ ܘܦܘܕܪ ܠܐ ܟܕܪܝܢ
I was beautiful since I was little.	W-mzoroothy khleetha wanwa	ܘܡܙܘܪܘܬܝ ܫܠܝܬܐ ܘܢܘܐ
You wanted to destroy my name,	B-aylakh d-makherwat shimmy	ܒܐܝܠܟ ܕܡܟܪܘܬ ܫܡܝ
and I didn't know what to do?	W-har ana ma awdanwa	ܘܗܪ ܐܢܐ ܡܐ ܐܘܕܢܘܐ
Your daughters always back you up.	B-nathakh dek-aray khasakh	ܒܢܬܟ ܕܟܐܪܝ ܚܣܟ
I was better than they were.	Bishto minnay wanwa	ܒܫܬܐ ܡܢܝ ܘܢܘܐ
They gossiped all night,	Layle koolleh bishlaba	ܠܝܠܐ ܟܘܠܗ ܒܫܠܒܐ
And didn't let me sleep."	La kshawqeewa d-damkhanwa	ܠܐ ܟܫܘܩܝܘܐ ܕܕܡܟܢܘܐ

الحمرة والبودر لا استعمل. من صغري كنت جميلة. حاولت أن تحطمي سمعتي ولم أستطع أن اعمل شيئا. كانت بناتك يتفقن معك. إنني كنت أجمل منهن. طوال الليل كنّ يثرثرن ولا يتركنني أن أنام.

(12)	(12)	(ܝܒ)
She said, "Why do you hate my daughters?	Bnathy qay k-sanyatay	ܒܢܬܝ ܩܝ ܟܣܢܝܬܝ
Why do you blow up at them?	W-qay k-ba-ajat min-ay	ܘܩܝ ܟܒܐܓܬ ܡܢܝ
Because they are better than you,	M-bay deelay bishto minnakh	ܡܒܝ ܕܝܠܝ ܒܫܬܐ ܡܢܟ
Quietly settled in their homes.	Teewe w-steere b-baythayi	ܛܝܘܐ ܘܣܛܝܪܐ ܒܒܝܬܝ

All the people love them,	Koollay nashe keebalay	ܟܠܠܝ ܢܫܐ ܟܐܒܠܝ
And they are remembered in a good way.	W-btawta kmathay bahsayi	ܘܒܬܘܬܐ ܟܡܬܝ ܒܚܣܝ
It kills you inside because	W-ayat k-harsat m-gawayihye	ܘܐܝܬ ܟܚܪܣܬ ܡܓܘܝܗܝܐ
They are loved by their husbands."	Bi-ayaylay mgooranahi	ܒܐܝܐܝܠܝ ܡܓܘܪܢܗܝ

لماذا تكرهين بناتي. ولماذا تتزعجين منهنّ. هل لأنّهنّ محبوبات من أزواجهنّ وجالسات مستورات في دورهنّ. كل الناس يحبونهنّ ويذكرون اسمهنّ بالخير. وأنت تنطقّين من الداخل لأنهنّ محبوبات من أزواجهنّ.

(13)	(13)	(ܝܓ)
She said, "I don't hate your daughters.	An bnathakh La k-sanyanay	ܐܢ ܒܢܬܟ ܠܐ ܟܣܢܝܢܝ
They mean nothing to me.	Laylay choo mimndi tali	ܠܝܠܝ ܟܘ ܡܡܢܕܝ ܬܠܝ
They speak evil to my husband to insult me,	K-athay kim harky gory	ܟܐܬܝ ܟܡ ܗܪܟܝ ܓܘܪܝ
In addition, my mother and sister.	Dimsa-er yimmi w-khathy	ܘܡܢܙܝܕܐ ܝܡܝ ܘܚܬܝ
Then you watch and rejoice.	Aigaha k-khayrat w-kpas-khat	ܐܝܓܗܐ ܟܚܝܪܬ ܘܟܦܣܚܬ
You raise my temperature.	K-mazidat elli shathy	ܟܡܙܝܕܬ ܐܠܝ ܫܬܝ
And I wish in my heart that	W-ana k-talbanwa blibby	ܘܐܢܐ ܟܬܠܒܢܘܐ ܒܠܒܝ
My mother-in-law's stomach is tied in knots."	D-araylah synpa khmathy	ܕܐܪܝܠܗ ܣܝܢܦܐ ܚܡܬܝ

إني لا أبغض بناتك. لأنهنّ لا شيئا بالنسبة إليّ. إنهنّ يأتين ويحرّكن زوجي ليسبّ أمي وأختي. وأنت تنظرين وتفرحين وتضاعفين الحمّى فيّ. وانا كنت أتمنى في قلبي بان يستولي الألم حماتي.

(14)	(14)	(ܝܕ)
After blaming each other,	Bather an dardamyatha	ܒܬܪ ܐܢ ܕܪܕܡܝܬܐ
fighting and bickering,	W-sharratha w-qal-ayatha	ܘܫܪܬܐ ܘܩܠܝܬܐ

family and friends gathered	Jmi-alay khoore w-nashwatha	ܓܡܝܥܠܗ ܚܘܪܐ ܘܢܫܘܬܗܐ
To bring peace to the home.	Tad daray shlama b-baytha	ܗܕ ܕܕܪܝ ܫܠܡܐ ܒܒܝܬܐ
They went to church	Zillay bighdade l-aayta	ܙܠܝ ܒܓܕܕܐ ܠܥܝܬܐ
To get advice from the priest.	Dshaqly min qasha masharta	ܕܫܩܠܝ ܡܢ ܩܫܐ ܡܫܪܬܐ
The bride, the groom, and the mother-in-law,	Kaloo w-khithna w-khmatha	ܟܠܘ ܘܚܬܢܐ ܘܚܡܬܐ
Entered the church frightened.	A-wayray l-aayta bizdotha	ܐܘܝܪܝ ܠܥܝܬܐ ܒܙܕܘܬܐ

بعد إلقاء اللوم على بعضهم البعض والقتال والتشاجر. اجتمع الأصدقاء والأهل ليضعوا السلام في الدار. ذهبوا سوية إلى الكنيسة لكي يستشيروا الخوري. الحماة والزوج والكنّة. دخلوا إلى دائرة الكنيسة خائفين.

(15)	(15)	(ܝܗ)
The priest said to them, "Come and sit.	Qasha mayreh hayo itwoo	ܩܫܐ ܡܝܪܗ ܗܝܘ ܝܬܘܘ
Enough of what you are doing.	Bassa m-mindi dkodootoo	ܒܣܐ ܡܡܢܕܝ ܕܟܕܘܬܘ
You are giving a bad example	Mathla beesha kyawootoo	ܡܬܠܐ ܒܝܫܐ ܟܝܘܘܬܘ
To all the young people.	Ta jooanqe kimshakootoo	ܗܐ ܠܥܘܢܩܐ ܟܡܫܟܘܬܘ
You have forgetten the love of the Lord	Hoobba d-maran k-nashotoo	ܚܘܒܐ ܕܡܪܢ ܟܢܫܘܬܘ
go to live in harmony and peace,	B-shayna w-shlama d-ayshootoo	ܒܫܝܢܐ ܘܫܠܡܐ ܕܥܝܫܘܬܘ
and show everyone	W- ta kool nashe d-makhwootoo	ܘܗܐ ܟܠ ܐܢܫܐ ܕܡܟܚܘܬܘ
You are true Christians."	M-haqa msheehaye wotoo	ܡܚܩܐ ܡܫܝܚܝܐ ܘܬܘ

خوري الكنيسة قال: تعالوا اجلسوا. يكفي ما تعملون. إنكم تعطون مثالا سيئا. وتشكّكون الشباب. نسيتم محبة الرب. وان تعيشوا بالهدوء والسلام. وتعطوا المثال الصالح لكل الناس. وتبرهنوا بانكم مسيحيون حقيقيون.

(16)	(16)	(ﻢﻫ)
The mother-in-law started to cry	Khmatha pishla bibkhaya	ܚܡܵܬ݂ܵܐ ܦܝܼܫܠܵܗ ܒܒܸܟ݂ܵܝܵܐ
As she kissed her daughter-in-law.	W-nshaqta l-kaloo bihwala	ܘܢܫܸܩܬܵܐ ܠܟܲܠܘܿ ܒܗܘܵܠܵܐ
The daughter-in-law's tears begin to fall.	W-kaloo dim-aah bijraya	ܘܟܲܠܘܿ ܕܡܲܥܵܗ ܒܓ݂ܵܪܵܝܵܐ
She got up and was reconciled with her mother-in-law.	Qimlah likhmathah m-soolhalah	ܩܝܼܡܠܵܗ ܠܝܼܚܡܵܬ݂ܵܗ ܡܨܘܼܠܚܲܠܵܗ
Everyone was happy to see that,	Koollay psykhlay l-dath hala	ܟܠܲܝ ܦܨܝܼܚܠܲܝ ܠܕܵܐܗ ܫܟ݂ܠܵܐ
Moreover, they all went straight home.	W-dayray l-baytha dla hmala	ܘܕܝܪܲܝ ܠܒܲܝܬ݂ܵܐ ܕܠܵܐ ܗܡܵܠܵܐ
The bride and the groom cheered	Khithna w-kaloo b-hoolala	ܚܸܬ݂ܢܵܐ ܘܟܲܠܘܿ ܒܗܘܿܠܵܠܵܐ
As happily as they did on The day of their wedding.	Ikh day-gid yoma d-koolala	ܐܝܼܟ݂ ܕܝܼܓܝܼܕ ܝܘܿܡܵܐ ܕܟܘܼܠܵܠܵܐ

الحماة بدأت تبكي وأخذت تقبّل الكنّة. والكنّة بدورها أخذت دموعها تنزل. فقامت وصالحت الحماة. كلهم فرحوا بهذه الحالة. ورجعوا إلى دارهم من دون توقّف. والعروس والعريس يهتفون كما في يوم زواجهم

SOME STATISTICS

Tilkepe: Between 1500-1900, Tilkepe was among the largest Chaldean Christian villages in the region. The census of 1868 stated that the population of Tilkepe reached 500 families. In the year 1900, the population was eight thousand people.

When the number of people in Iraq in the beginning of twentieth century was seven million, the population of Tilkepe was approximately ten thousand people.

After the First World War in 1915, Tilkepe received Christians who fled from Armenia, Georgia, Turkey, Hakkari Mountains, Diyarbakir and Mardin. After the Second World War, more Christians were received from the Amadiyah, Duhok, and Zakho.

In the sixties and seventies of the twentieth century, the number of Christians in Tilkepe reached about 850 families divided between the Chaldean indigenous Catholics and the Chaldean Catholics who immigrated to it from the North, among the members of the Eastern Church, with its two branches. In 1991, the population was 900 families.

In 2007, the population of Tilkepe reached 500 families, while the Tilkepnaye in diaspora reached more than 50,000 people. According to the official census carried out in 2013, the population of Tilkepe was 1,800. The percentage of Christians was only 22%. Prior to the displacement in 2014, there were 950 families in Tilkepe; only about 50 Christian families returned. These returning families consisted of Chaldean indigenous Catholics, and families from the Assyrian Church of the East, Mart Shmouni, the ancient Church of the East, the Church of Mar Shimaon Bar Sabayi, and some Syriac families.

In the last quarter of the twentieth century, Tilkepe had recovered economically. Plaster factories and production of tahini and bulgur had increased. Al-Hallan (marble stone) was cut and exported to other cities, even outside the country, especially to the Gulf countries.

Since the beginning of the twentieth century, the number of Christians has begun to shrink. The number of Muslims is doubling. Tilkepnaye were subjected to Arabization. The lands were distributed to Bedouins and government officials from abroad. As a result, Tilkepe became an Arab region par excellence. Most of the factories and projects stalled and eventually closed. Even non-Chaldeans relied on the money sent from their families.

Here is the latest news from Tilkepe. On January 23, 2020, a marathon was launched. The goal of the marathon was to promote peace between the residents of Tilkepe, under the slogan "There is no path to peace. Peace is the path."

The Tilkepe District, specifically the Tilkepe Youth Center Stadium, witnessed, for the first time in Nineveh Governorate, a course on skateboarding for a number of Tilkepe children and young women.. The course started on Sunday February 9, 2020, and lasted for five days.

The Diocese of Mosul celebrated the laying of the hand of His Excellency Mar Mikhael Naguib, the head of the diocese, by granting the deacon degree to the clerical Shaker Yohanan Zaitouna, who was born in Tilkepe, in 1963. The bishop also granted deacon Shaker the degree of priesthood on January 15th, 2021 in Tilkepe.

From the beginning of the nineteenth century until today, Christians, especially the people of Tilkepe, went through harsh conditions and they left from all cities in the country. Then they journeyed, searching for religious and social freedom overseas, especially to America. When conditions allowed them, they sent for their relatives and friends, and their numbers reached the thousands. Some people even estimate the number of Tilkepnaye living abroad to be more than fifty thousand. Wherever they are, they spread love and goodwill. They cherish their parents' Chaldean language.

Those who wish to know more about them can go to the records of Benefactors in most churches in Iraq, Europe and Canada, and more in America. In the famous words of His Beatitude, the patriarch Mar Polos Cheikho, "Before you decided to build a church or establish a project, ask how many Tilkepnaye reside in the area."

Wherever Tilkepnaye landed, they engaged in religious, economic and political work. Tilkepnaye have occupied the top positions in trade, finance and administration. Their relations were cordial with the custodians of the rest of the Christian villages, including intermarriage and economic relations, and most importantly, the association of sect and religion, where everyone is a Catholic. At the same time, good relations have existed between Tilkepnaye and Assyrian and Syriac villages.

As with non-Christians, there were commercial relations, as Tilkepnaye were trading with the Kurds (Macroye) continuously, carrying what they needed and buying from them charcoal, raisins and fruits, as well as grains, such as rice, sesame and wheat. Tilkepe lost many young men to thieves while trading on the way to the mountain (north) where the Kurdish people lived. It is worth noting that some of the Tilkepnaye opened shops in the northern villages, and the rest of the family lived there and with the Arabs, grazed sheep and other commercial matters.

Although property and possessions were taken over by strangers; nevertheless, we have to love our country, from where we were raised, and from it, we draw our history. Tilkepnaye must never forget their heritage.

Do you ever see a day when some of us would return to our beloved Tilkepe, which is kept in our hearts tomorrow to be seen soon?

Other Titles by Let in the Light Publishing:

- A High School Tennis Coach's Handbook:
  For Players, Parents, and Coaches
- Aramaic Language Chaldean Dialogue
- Beginner's Handbook of the Aramaic Chaldean
  Alphabets
- Chaldeans Present and Past Classical Aramaic I
- Classical Aramaic II
- Preserving the Chaldean Aramaic Language
- Read and Write the Modern Aramaic
- The Advanced Handbook of Modern Aramaic Dialect
- Tilkepe Past and Present
- Who are the Chaldeans?
- The Life of Tilkepnaye was also published in a trilingual paperback
  edition containing English, Arabic, and Aramaic translations.

To order, please visit: www.letinthelightpublishing.com.
Let in the Light looks forward to serving you!

Acknowledgments

I appreciate the help of Mr. Jimmy Akin. He provided the task of ensuring constancy between the Aramaic and English portion of the text, thus making it more accessible to a broader audience. Many thanks to Brenda Sako for her effort and contribution in reviewing the final English portion of this book.

Note: All the photos in this book are taken from 1964-1972, the time I served in my hometown of Tilkepe.

August 20, 2020

About the Author

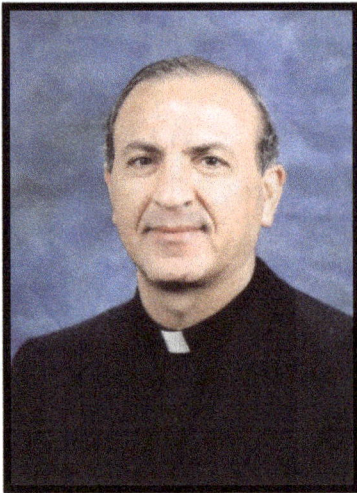

Fr. Michael J. Bazzi (Emeritus) was born in Tilkepe, Iraq in 1938 to Catholic parents. In 1954, he entered St. Peter's Catholic Seminary in Mosul, Iraq. After 10 years he was ordained a priest in Baghdad on May 15, 1964. He served in Tilkepe from 1964-1972. As assistant priest, he worked with youth, establishing Bible study groups. Bazzi published Tilkepe: Present and Past in Arabic in 1969. From 1972-1974 he studied Pastoral Theology in Rome at the Lateran University. Bazzi received a Master's degree in Pastoral Theology as well as diplomas in Mass Media and Group Dynamics.

Arriving in the United States on June 20, 1974, Bazzi taught scripture for five years in Oshkosh, Wisconsin (Greenbay Diocese) and four years in Michigan, where he established two churches. In 1983, he moved to Los Angeles where he served as a pastor of St. Paul's parish in Montrose and on September 1, 1985, Bazzi moved to San Diego and became assistant pastor at St. Peter's Parish. In 1987, Fr. Bazzi became pastor of St. Peter Parish. He worked with adults and youth, establishing Bible Study groups and teaching Catechism and Aramaic language in its Chaldean dialect. In 1989, he established St. Michael's Chaldean Catholic parish in El Cajon. At St. Peter's Parish he had established three projects for the community:
1) St. Peter Church Hall 2) Education Center 3) The large rectory.

Professor Bazzi has been teaching the Chaldean Dialect of Aramaic Language at Cuyamaca College since 1989. Bazzi has published several textbooks on modern and classical Aramaic including: *Classical Aramaic I & II, Modern Aramaic Vol. I & II, Beginners Handbook of the Aramaic Language*, a children's book called *Read and Write Aramaic*, the divine liturgy with parallel *Aramaic-Chaldean Dialect, Know Your Faith*, and *Who are the Chaldeans?*

www.ingramcontent.com/pod-product-compliance
Lightning Source LLC
Chambersburg PA
CBHW050618110426
42813CB00008B/2599